# A Woman's
# BODY
# Balanced by
# Nature

❧

## JANET MACCARO, PHD, CNC

## SILOAM

Most CHARISMA HOUSE BOOK GROUP products are available at special quantity discounts for bulk purchase for sales promotions, premiums, fund-raising, and educational needs. For details, write Charisma House Book Group, 600 Rinehart Road, Lake Mary, Florida 32746, or telephone (407) 333-0600.

A WOMAN'S BODY BALANCED BY NATURE by Janet Maccaro, PhD, CNC
Published by Siloam
Charisma Media/Charisma House Book Group
600 Rinehart Road
Lake Mary, Florida 32746
www.siloam.com

Scripture quotations marked NKJV are from the New King James Version of the Bible. Copyright © 1979, 1980, 1982 by Thomas Nelson, Inc., publishers. Used by permission.

Scripture quotations marked THE MESSAGE are from *The Message: The Bible in Contemporary English*, copyright © 1993, 1994, 1995, 1996, 2000, 2001, 2002. Used by permission of NavPress Publishing Group.

Cover design by Bill Johnson and Judith McKittrick
Interior design by Terry Clifton

Library of Congress Cataloging-in-Publication Data:
Maccaro, Janet C.
A woman's body balanced by nature / Janet Maccaro.
    p. cm.
ISBN 1-59185-968-9 (hard back)
1. Women--Health and hygiene--Popular works. I. Title.

RA778.M136 2006
613'.04244--dc22

                                    2006014571
ISBN 13: 978-1-59185-968-0

Neither the publisher nor the author is engaged in rendering professional advice or services to the individual reader. The ideas, procedures, and suggestions in this book are not intended as a substitute for consulting with your physician. All matters regarding your health require medical supervision. Neither the author nor the publisher shall be liable or responsible for any loss or damage allegedly arising from any information or suggestion in this book.

The recipes in this book are to be followed exactly as written. The publisher is not responsible for your specific health or allergy needs that may require medical supervision. The publisher is not responsible for any adverse reactions to the recipes contained in this book.

While the author has made every effort to provide accurate telephone numbers and Internet addresses at the time of publication, neither the publisher nor the author assumes any responsibility for errors or for changes that occur after publication.

16 17 18 19 20 — 98765432
Printed in the United States of America

Balance.

Why does it elude us? Can women juggle their lives with the same expertise of a circus performer without sacrificing their current and future state of health? The answer is yes, provided they understand that successful juggling requires balance.

This body of work is dedicated to mothers, daughters, sisters, and friends who realize that life is a continual *balancing act*. When one woman balances her life, she has a balancing effect on the lives of all the women she knows and loves.

The key to *VIBRANT HEALTH* is all in the *BALANCE*!

# ACKNOWLEDGMENTS

A special thanks to Barbara Dycus, my editor, advocate, and friend during the creation of *A Woman's Body Balanced by Nature*.

# CONTENTS

There is a balance in nature so delicately and intricately interdependent that it is beyond the scope of our understanding. Yet, when that balance is lost, we can immediately see the result. As rainfall decreases, aquatic plants die due to lowered water levels, fish die because of poor oxygenation, animals on the water's edge leave or die from starvation, and insect populations increase as birds and other natural feeders leave the ecosystem, leaving it desolate and compromised. The same holds true for a woman's body. Once balance is lost, her quality of life is never the same. She ceases to flourish, and her dreams of vibrant and abundant health are replaced with fatigue, loss of mental clarity, anxiety, depression, and degenerative disease.

For nearly twenty years I searched to regain my balance, with all systems of my body working in harmony and vibrancy. I suffered from systemic yeast infection, Epstein-Barr virus, rheumatic fever, mitral valve prolapse, heart murmur, low blood sugar, strep infections, endometriosis with resultant hysterectomy, asthma, and devastating panic attacks. Finding my balance required addressing the foundational needs of my body, my mind, and my spirit.

I liken it to replenishing the water in a pond, which will bring back vegetation...which brings back the fish...which brings back the wildlife—all intricately balanced, all dependent upon one another in order to flourish and thrive. Once my body was balanced, I felt at one with all of God's creation, vibrant, productive, an active participant, reaching out to other women who were trapped in a body out of balance.

The purpose of this book is to offer you practical advice based upon my personal twenty-year journey from chronic illness to vibrant health, as well as research on nontoxic alternatives for dealing with health problems women face throughout their lives, from the cradle to the grave. I offer you natural, herbal, and holistic alternatives for balancing your body, mind, and spirit, and thereby preventing disease.

It is a labor of love and a subject that is very close to my heart. As a woman, I know that I am part of a family of women whose numbers are immeasurable. The health choices we make as the result of informed health decisions will affect the health and well-being of generations of women who follow. I sense immense responsibility to inform, educate, share, and empower you with the tools needed to live your best life—now.

This book is a culmination of my life's work. It provides a look at how a woman—every woman—can achieve total balance in her body physically, emotionally, and spiritually. Because this book provides a complete look at a woman's health, parts of it have been adapted from my previous books, each of which covered specific areas of a woman's health. This book is intended to be very interactive, because I believe that when women participate in their wellness, they regain balance more rapidly. You will be given health surveys and screenings, complete with natural protocols and education on health issues that all women share.

Think of this book as your personal owner's manual, written especially for your body, complete with troubleshooting tips for hormonal health, beauty, weight control, anxiety, depression, relationship issues, and anything that we as women encounter in this life.

It has been said that every woman who is healed helps to heal all of the women who came before her and all of those who will come after her.[1] As a woman brings balance to her life physically, emotionally, and spiritually, she literally fertilizes and replenishes the soil out of which future generations of women grow. A woman who has achieved balance is free from anxiety, depression, worry, and physical maladies. Sleep comes, vibrancy abounds, and all lives are enriched by her wisdom and ability to weather life's storms with grace and dignity.

A balanced woman is a treasure to behold. Her beauty transcends the physical realm. Her strength and insight shine forth as a beacon to others. Her body, mind, and spirit function in concert. She walks in abundant and divine health.

A balanced woman gives and nurtures unconditionally, but at the same time, she knows the love she gives so freely needs to be given to herself as well. She knows that she is worthy of love and care. This body of work is written especially for women who are willing to give themselves that love and care. A woman's body, when in balance, allows her to be the full expression of what God designed her to be! Finding your balance is worth the effort. You are worth it!

## HOW TO USE THIS BOOK

You will begin this book in chapter one by completing important self-assessment health screenings to show you how your current lifestyle is affecting your current state of health. I will then educate you on the systems that help a woman's body to function in balance. Our goal in the first chapter is to help you to know your body—its needs physically, emotionally, and spiritually. Where are your strengths and weaknesses? Where does your body need strengthening? What relationships in your life are healthy? And which ones are draining you and aging you more quickly than necessary?

Once you become educated on the *whys* and *hows* of your current state of imbalance and are armed with a working plan of action, we will move forward to discover all the ingredients necessary for a balanced, vibrant life now! Chapters two through eleven contain ten essential building blocks to balance your body, mind, and spirit. These keys include:

---

### THE KEYS TO BALANCE

- *Women's nutrition*: Establishing nutritional balance
- *Nutritional supplements*: Understanding the vitamins and supplements important for balance
- *Weight control*: Learning to control your weight
- *Exercise*: Recognizing the role of exercise for balance physically, emotionally, and spiritually

- ✧ *Sleep*: Discovering the recuperative effects of sleep
- ✧ *Beauty*: Finding true beauty—naturally
- ✧ *Antiaging*: Learning important antiaging protocols
- ✧ *Hormones*: Fitting together the pieces of hormonal balance
- ✧ *Stress*: Reducing the stress that robs you of balance
- ✧ *Relationships*: Discovering the power of positive relationships in your life

As you learn to use these ten important building blocks for balance, you will begin to prepare your body for lifelong balance, physically, mentally, and spiritually. Once you are equipped with this information, you will be ready to deal with the imbalance that has been robbing you of vibrant health.

It has been said that "the whole world is a stage," and I believe that nature serves as a "backdrop." Just like all things in nature, each one of us has a part in this play we call *life*. To play your part well, you *must* get your *act together*. This is where balance comes in. The key to a great performance in life is to achieve balance—body, mind, and spirit.

*JP Marcoao PhD CNC*

CHAPTER 1
## KNOW YOUR BODY

Let me congratulate you on taking the first step in balancing your body naturally. You are setting aside time for YOU! This is a very good thing!

If you are a woman who is suffering from imbalances in your system, it becomes hard for you to truly reach your divine potential. This can be a source of frustration and depression when not dealt with. A woman's body is delicately balanced. Even subtle imbalances can severely impact the quality of your daily life.

In an effort to reach thousands of women in this country who are dealing with a plethora of symptoms that seem to elude even the best of diagnosticians, I offer this guide, complete with protocols to balance your body now and for years to come. Let this be your reference, or blueprint, to help you maintain your balance once it is achieved. Share it with your mother, daughter, sister, and best friend. It is a gift I give to you. I have lived in a body out of balance. I know the anguish and the pain, the anxiety, and the discouragement and feelings of hopelessness that occur as a result. I also know what balance regained feels like. I can attest…there is nothing like it! So, that being said, let's begin!

There are three essentials of balance:

THE TEN ESSENTIAL BUILDING BLOCKS

- *Body*—Balance the body using nutrients that are specific for detoxifying, balancing, and strengthening the systems of the body.

- *Mind*—Make a conscious choice to be well, taking the time and effort to heal past and present emotional wounds. Practice forgiveness, and develop an attitude of gratitude on a daily basis.

- *Spirit*—Develop and maintain a personal relationship with your Creator. Nurture your soul, for you are a spiritual being having an earthly experience!

If you neglect to balance all three of these areas, true balance becomes impossible.

Let's begin with your physical body. The first section of this chapter deals with the essentials for achieving balance when it comes to your physical health.

## THE BODY—TAKING INVENTORY OF YOUR PHYSICAL BODY

To begin the process of balancing your body, you must first take inventory of your current state of health. I am going to ask you a series of questions targeted to the different systems of your body. Your answers will help to determine where you need assistance and balancing. The accuracy of your answers is crucial. Your reward will be a higher level of health! Balance does not mean to simply seek to suppress your symptoms, but rather it means to discover and eliminate the root cause of your imbalance.

Let's examine your body by observing its eight main systems: the gastrointestinal, structural/neurological, cardiovascular, immune, respiratory, genitourinary, eyes and ears, and endocrine/glandular.

My goal is to educate you by involving you in your own health care. By doing so you will become an active participant in your personal well-being. You will learn to be more accountable for your dietary lifestyle. You will also learn that imbalance can be the result of emotional unrest or spiritual depletion. Emphasis on emotional and spiritual renewal is an important component in the balancing process.

Several checks in any given area or section will alert you to focus your attention on that particular system. Remember, when one system is out of balance, it affects the other systems. Just like a team of horses, if one horse is weak or cannot pull its weight, the other horses have to pick up the slack and become overtaxed. The same holds true for your body. Balance is key. After taking the screenings, you will know what system to focus upon and strengthen.

While overcoming my personal health struggles, my studies took me on a journey through all avenues of alternative medicine. In Chinese medicine I found it is believed that if you have moved into chronic illness of any kind, a balancing principle must be applied. This is where balancing all the systems of your body comes into play. This balancing is known as the principle of regeneration. Regeneration differs from medicine because it has nothing at all to do with disease. To treat a disease, medicine first names it, then seeks a specific cure for it. The regeneration principle, in contrast, holds that there are no specific diseases, only internal weaknesses, usually reversible, that manifest in certain symptomatic patterns. By using the symptomatic pattern to discern the weakness, and then strengthening the body system, we create optimal conditions that allow the symptoms to go away, replaced by the vitality and balance of health. The regeneration principle was a blessing to my physical body. I am excited to share it with you because my goal is to help you discover and live principles of healthful living that will restore balance to your body, mind, and spirit.

Keep firmly in mind that you must shift your thinking from the disease-oriented point of view where you seek an external cure for a specific disease to a regeneration principle where you seek to strengthen and balance your body, paying attention to symptoms only as signs of possible weakness. Vitamins, medicines, herbs, potions, lotions, and the like heal nothing! Your body is designed with the God-given ability to heal. Support the body, strengthen the weak areas, and let the healing begin!

THE TEN ESSENTIAL BUILDING BLOCKS

## Know Your Body Self-Assessment Screening

It is imperative that you take inventory of your body and see just where your weaknesses are. You may find that some of your complaints seem to run in your family or are hereditary. Don't let this alarm you. This simply means that those weak areas need more attention or strengthening.

## Your Gastrointestinal System

Do you experience any of the following:

- ☐ Stomach pain
- ☐ Fatigue after eating
- ☐ Frequent heartburn
- ☐ Frequent constipation
- ☐ Irritable bowel syndrome
- ☐ Hemorrhoids
- ☐ Vomiting
- ☐ Colitis
- ☐ Gallbladder trouble
- ☐ Frequent burping/belching
- ☐ Nausea
- ☐ Ulcers

## Your Structural/Neurological System

Do you experience:

- ☐ Headaches
- ☐ Muscle cramps
- ☐ Neck pain
- ☐ Jaw pain
- ☐ Dizziness
- ☐ Back pain

- [ ] Shoulder/elbow, wrist pain
- [ ] Knee/hip pain
- [ ] Joint pain or loss of function
- [ ] Osteoporosis or osteomalacia
- [ ] Tendonitis/bursitis

## YOUR CARDIOVASCULAR SYSTEM

Do you experience:

- [ ] Irregular heartbeat
- [ ] Heart murmur/palpitations
- [ ] High or low blood pressure
- [ ] Chest pain
- [ ] Poor circulation
- [ ] Previous heart surgery
- [ ] Varicose or spider veins
- [ ] Cold hands and feet

## YOUR IMMUNE SYSTEM

Which symptoms of low immunity have you experienced?

- [ ] Frequently sick
- [ ] Swollen glands/sore throats
- [ ] Depression and/or anxiety
- [ ] Achy joints/muscle pain
- [ ] Headaches/migraines
- [ ] Recurrent digestive complaints
- [ ] Chronic fatigue
- [ ] Food allergies
- [ ] Eczema or hives
- [ ] Allergies

## YOUR RESPIRATORY SYSTEM

Check the appropriate boxes:

☐ Chronic cough

☐ Asthma

☐ Emphysema

☐ Recurrent head colds

☐ Recurrent sinus problems

☐ Recurrent bronchitis

☐ Are you a smoker?

## Your Genitourinary Tract

Check the appropriate boxes:

☐ Too frequent urination

☐ Blood in your urine

☐ Recurrent kidney or bladder problems

☐ Kidney stones

☐ Inability to control bladder

## Eyes and Ears

Check the appropriate boxes:

☐ Recurrent ear infections

☐ Eye infections

☐ Floaters in your eyes

☐ Glaucoma

☐ Macular degeneration

☐ Cataracts

## Your Endocrine/Glandular System

Check the appropriate boxes:

☐ Cold hands and feet

☐ Low blood pressure

☐ Weight problems, over or under

☐ Thyroid problems

☐ Diabetes

☐ Irritability if meals are missed

☐ Dizzy upon standing too quickly

☐ Depression

☐ Frequent headaches

☐ Digestive complaints

☐ Recurrent urinary tract infections

☐ Yeast infections

☐ Menstrual irregularity

☐ Cramping

☐ Mood swings/depression

☐ Premenstrual syndrome

☐ Infertility

☐ Frequent miscarriages

☐ Hot flashes

☐ Currently taking hormone medications

☐ Currently taking birth control pills

☐ Lumps in your breast

☐ Uterine fibroids/ovarian cysts

☐ Leaky bladder

☐ Endometriosis

Each of these systems will be discussed in this chapter, and you will find additional information and protocols that will address your symptoms throughout the ten essential building blocks for achieving balance. As you read each chapter, refer back to the boxes you checked, applying the protocols I give you to overcome that symptom of imbalance in your life.

## A WOMAN'S GASTROINTESTINAL SYSTEM

A woman's gastrointestinal system is delicately balanced and can be disrupted by stress, both good and bad, which can lead to emotional overeating or poor food choices or combinations, such as fried, fatty, or sugary foods that can slow down transit time and lead to constipation. Bowel flora imbalance and digestive enzyme deficiency can create uncomfortable bloating and gas.

Many women look forward to spring as a time to clean their homes from top to bottom, sweeping out all of the dirt, dust, and cobwebs from the previous season. If you are feeling dull, draggy, and run-down, you may be tired and toxic. It is time for you to give your system a *spring cleaning* from top to bottom!

Before you begin to balance your body, I recommend that you detoxify or cleanse your system. Any woman who is experiencing tiredness may instead be toxic. The headaches, aches and pains, sinus problems, weight problems, foggy-headed feeling, intestinal gas, irregularity, and indigestion may be warning signs indicating a need for detoxification.

More and more evidence points to the accumulation of toxins as the cause of accelerated aging and chronic diseases. Our generation has been exposed to more pollution than any other generation in history. By the time we reach midlife, we have consumed pounds of sugar, gallons of caffeinated beverages, and too many processed and fast foods to count. Add in medications and the fact that we have not eaten with any sort of balance due to our hectic lifestyles, coupled with a lack of fresh fruits and vegetables and not enough fiber to help move these toxins out of our systems, and you have the makings of *autointoxification* or *self-poisoning*. This occurs when the toxic buildup is so great that it recycles and enters the bloodstream, causing a myriad of uncomfortable symptoms that often baffle the very best physicians.

Clearing toxins from the body is an important self-care procedure that should be a part of your preventative health care. Why are we so toxic? Considering all of the steroids, antibiotics, pesticides, waxes, hormones, dyes, and waxes used in and on our food supply, it is no wonder that these materials set off reactions in the body that can cause a variety of health problems. Toxicity can cause frequent illness, make us look older than our years, and rob us of our vitality.

Many doctors and researchers now agree that degenerative conditions of the heart, colon, joints, and kidneys, as well as dizziness, depression, arthritis, insomnia, and immune suppression, may be the result of toxic accumulation in the body. Our eliminative ability slows down as a result of this toxicity, which is combined with the manufacture of our own bodily wastes.

*Dr. Janet's Recommendation:*

*Nature's Secret Ultimate Cleanse*, available in most health food stores, is a very effective whole-body cleansing formula.

Our bodies become a virtual storehouse of pollutants. As a result, we begin to have poor nutrient absorption because our polluted intestines cannot properly screen out chemicals or adequately filter food particles.

This allows toxins to enter the bloodstream, sometimes even leading to "leaky gut" or irritable bowel syndrome. If you are not eliminating properly—which means having two to three bowel movements per day, each and every day—you are constipated. This gives the toxic wastes a chance to enter the bloodstream and create chronic unwellness or low energy. You have twenty-seven feet of intestinal tract. If you eat three meals a day, plus snacks, just think of what occurs if you do not eliminate properly. Think of the amount of toxicity that builds as the food stagnates, ferments, and becomes putrefied. Not a pleasant picture, but this is an illustration that you need in order to drive home the importance of cleansing your internal system.

One way to rectify this problem is to cleanse your system twice a year, in the spring and the fall. A very easy, user-friendly way to do this would be to use an herbal formula that contains time-tested synergistic herbs that are system specific, meaning herbs that cleanse the liver, blood, colon, and so forth. When you take ancient herbal wisdom and marry it with the formulating technology of today, you have the benefit of having a very efficient way to correct toxic overload and regain your health.

THE TEN ESSENTIAL BUILDING BLOCKS

When it comes to detoxification, there are ways to go other than herbal formulations, including colonics, fasting, saunas, enemas, and juicing. But for ease, convenience, and effectiveness, herbal cleansing has been found to be the most effective, provided you use a superior product. When it comes to the product you use, remember that formulation is key. It must not be too harsh, and it must not consist of laxative herbs only. Find a formulation that contains the system-specific herbs as well as the herbs that help sweep the colon for removal of toxins from your system. The process usually takes from thirty to ninety days to gently eliminate years of accumulated waste matter. To further enhance the process, make sure that you clean up your diet and drink plenty of good-quality water.

Many women feel as if they have been given their health back after detoxification. Their skin clears up, elimination is regular, eyes sparkle, energy soars, vitality returns, digestion improves, aches and pains diminish or disappear, headaches become a thing of the past, and unhealthy cravings disappear. When you consider all of these benefits, it is as if you have been given a clean slate or foundation from which to build your health to a higher, more vibrant level! You can take responsibility and do your part to help prevent some of the most debilitating diseases of our time. Become proactive—cleanse your body and add more life to your years!

In my journey toward wellness, detoxification played a large part in my recovery. I believe detoxification is essential when it comes to balancing your body. Clearing toxins from the body is a self-care procedure that is an important part of preventative health care.

### Achieving gastrointestinal balance

Let's begin the balancing act. Poor digestion can cause many of the symptoms that were listed in the self-assessment screening. It has many causative factors, including eating too fast or when stressed; eating too much; eating too many refined, acidic, fatty, and spicy foods; food sensitivities; allergies to wheat or dairy; and poor diet with overconsumption of sugar and poor elimination.

If you checked any of the symptoms for your gastrointestinal system in the Know Your Body Self-Assessment Screening at the beginning of this chapter, you should consider taking digestive enzymes from a plant source with every meal. We now live in a world where our foods are so microwaved, processed, nutrient poor, overcooked, and over-sugared that our own digestive enzymes, which are normally found in our digestive process, are often depleted by the enormous enzymatic workload they have to perform. Digestive enzymes are *crucial* for proper food assimilation. DicQie Fuller, in her informative book *The Healing Power of Enzymes*, has stated: "Any time we suffer from an acute or chronic illness, it is almost certain an enzyme depletion problem exists."[1]

Although mainstream medicine does not often recommend digestive enzymes to women with digestive disturbances, many physicians have heard less from their women patients once digestion is normalized by enzyme supplementation. Natural health practitioners believe that the first order of business, when it comes to alleviating digestive discomfort and restoring the health of the digestive tract, is to supplement with digestive enzymes. The *pink stuff* is just a cover-up! (See chapter three for more information on digestive enzyme supplementation.)

Did you check the box for *frequent heartburn*? Many cases of heartburn, acid reflux, and acid indigestion are the result of insufficient hydrochloric acid production in the stomach. Any time you experience insufficient stomach acid for proper digestion, food begins to ferment. Fermentation in the stomach creates gas. When your stomach expands from this gas, the gas travels upward toward the esophagus. As it continues to push into the esophagus, stomach acid enters with it. When stomach acid reaches the esophagus, a burning sensation occurs in the throat and creates heartburn. Natural medicine states that heartburn solutions must address the cause of the condition, which is insufficient hydrochloric acid. Over-the-counter antacids are sold to neutralize the stomach acid and provide relief. In reality, antacids actually compound digestive problems by neutralizing stomach acid. This is not conducive to a healthy digestive tract. When your stomach becomes less acidic, your system can become a welcoming home to bad bacteria, candida, parasites, and intestinal toxemia.[2]

If *constipation and hemorrhoids* are a problem, you should know that a poor diet plays a huge part in the development of these two conditions. Too little fiber, too many fried, sugar foods, and too much red meat, caffeine, and alcohol are the biggest culprits. Not drinking enough water (especially when traveling), lack of exercise, hypothyroidism, and the use of antidepressant drugs are major factors for women. Proper elimination is crucial for optimal health.

*Dr. Janet's Recommendation:*

Use Betaine HCL at mealtimes, which will help to insure that your stomach contains enough acid for proper digestion and relief of troublesome digestive disturbance symptoms.

### SIGNS OF POOR ELIMINATION AND TOXIC OVERLOAD

- Fatigue
- Irritability
- Headaches
- Mental dullness
- Gas
- Nausea
- Depression
- Coated tongue
- Bad breath
- Body odor
- Sallow skin

Another common condition that seems to strike women more often than men is *irritable bowel syndrome (IBS)*. This may be due to the fact that most contributing factors are common to the lifestyle of women today. Most IBS sufferers are women between the ages of twenty and forty years old, with A-type personalities and stressful jobs or lifestyles. Women who are anxious, tense, coffee drinkers, lactose sensitive, or women who have taken repeated courses of anti-inflammatory drugs or suffer from yeast overgrowth due to antibiotic use are most commonly afflicted.

*Colitis* is a very painful condition that develops in stages. It may begin with weakness, fatigue, and lethargy, and then be followed by abdominal cramps, distention, and pain, which are relieved by bowel movements. Soon a woman may experience recurrent constipation, alternating with bloody diarrhea and mucus in the stool. Rectal hemorrhoids, fistulas, and abscesses; dehydration; mineral loss; and unhealthy weight loss with abdominal distention occur as this condition progresses.

The good news is that the world of natural medicine has answers for all of the conditions mentioned above. You will find my healthy, natural protocols in the following chapters to guide you into better balance in these areas. The reward is vibrant health with plenty of energy! Keep in mind that natural remedies take as long as three to six months for you to have dramatic results. This is because natural medicine does not put a Band-Aid on or suppress symptoms. Rather, natural medicine seeks out the root cause of your distress and then supports the body by cleansing and detoxifying, nurturing, and balancing and rebuilding your system.

The following chart gives you dietary guidelines for the health conditions that may occur from gastrointestinal problems. More specific protocols will be found throughout the book.

### Steps to Gastrointestinal Health

- Eat smaller meals, and chew food well.
- Take a daily walk to stimulate regularity.
- Avoid antacids; often they neutralize HCL in the stomach.
- Reduce stress in your life.
- Clean up your diet by avoiding coffee, caffeinated foods, sodas, nuts, seeds, dairy, and citrus, especially while trying to heal from colitis.

THE TEN ESSENTIAL BUILDING BLOCKS

↩ Eliminate sugary foods, fried foods, sorbitol, and dairy foods (lactose intolerance often affects IBS sufferers). Eliminate wheat (another irritant), and avoid antibiotics, antacids, and milk of magnesia, which destroy friendly bacteria in the intestinal tract.

Can we talk? It is important to address the delicate subject of *elimination*. While elimination varies from woman to woman, it is important to know what *normal* is. For health to be optimal, you should be eliminating two to three times daily. A healthy bowel movement should be brown to light tan, light enough to float (indicating enough fiber intake), bulky, and easy to pass. A strong odor indicates toxicity, slow transit time, or a diet that is too high in animal proteins and saturated fat. As you clean up your diet (by adding fiber, rich whole grains, and fresh fruits and vegetables), you will see marked improvement.

I recommend that you enjoy some of the delicious herbal teas available to help with digestive problems. Peppermint tea, spearmint tea, and alfalfa mint tea are especially helpful to aid digestion.

### Quick Fixes From Nature

| Symptom | Remedy |
|---|---|
| Heartburn | Aloe vera juice |
| Sour stomach | Lime juice with a pinch of ginger |
| Bloating | ½ teaspoon baking soda in water |
| Poor absorption | Glass of wine with dinner |
| Flatulence | Slippery elm tea or as an enema; or cinnamon, nutmeg, ginger, and cloves in water |

*Gallbladder problems*

- Do you have intense pain in the upper right abdomen that is accompanied by nausea?
- Do you have recurring abdominal pain, bloating, and gas after you eat a heavy meal?
- Do you have spells of nausea, fever, vomiting, and intense abdominal pain that radiates to the upper back?

Women make up about three-fourths of the twenty million gallbladder disease sufferers in America.[3] If you suffer from high cholesterol, chronic indigestion, gas, or obesity, or if you are a yo-yo dieter or consume too much dairy and refined sugary foods, you are at risk. Improving your diet is the key in the prevention of gallbladder disease and the formation of gallstones.

Reduce your intake of animal protein, especially dairy foods, and avoid fried and fatty foods, sugary foods, and fast foods. Increase your fresh fruit and vegetable intake because they contain fiber. Fiber keeps bad cholesterol deposits from forming and keeps food moving through your system properly. If you have gallstones, you may want to consider doing a gallbladder/liver flush. I have personally done several of these flushes. Each time I am amazed at the results. If you suspect that you have large gallstones, I must recommend that you have a sonogram *before* you embark on this procedure, because the gallstones *must* be small enough to pass through the bile duct during the flush. If the stones are too large, they must be dissolved first by using Stone-X (available at most health food stores). Seek out a nutritionally aware health-care provider, and work with that person so you can be monitored.

### GALLBLADDER/LIVER FLUSH

The liver and gallbladder flush is an important detoxifying procedure that may help restore the normal functional capacity of these organs.

THE TEN ESSENTIAL BUILDING BLOCKS

1. Monday through Saturday noon, drink as much apple juice or apple cider as your appetite will permit in addition to your regular meals and any supplements that you regularly take. The apple juice should be unfiltered and free of additives and preservatives. You may find it at your local health food store.
2. At noon on Saturday, you should eat a normal lunch.
3. Three hours later, take 2 teaspoons of Epsom salts in about 2 ounces of water. The taste will be objectionable to you and therefore may be followed by a little fresh-squeezed citrus juice. (Grapefruit juice is ideal.)
4. Two hours later, repeat step 3.
5. You may have grapefruit or other citrus juice for your evening meal.
6. At bedtime, you may have one of the following:
   —One-half cup of unrefined olive oil followed by a small glass of grapefruit juice
   —One-half cup of warm, unrefined olive oil blended with ½ cup of lemon juice.

   Unrefined olive oil can be purchased from any health food store. It is best to use fresh citrus juice, but canned or bottled is allowed. Use a blender to whip the oil and the juice together. This will improve the taste and the texture. Use a straw to drink the mixture.
7. Following step 6, you should go to bed immediately and lie on your right side with your right knee pulled close to your chest for thirty minutes.
8. One hour before breakfast the next morning, take 2 teaspoons of Epsom salts dissolved in 2 ounces of hot water.
9. Be sure to continue with your normal diet and any nutritional supplements that you normally take, except for the evening that you do step 6.

Some women report slight to moderate nausea when taking the olive oil/citrus juice combo. This nausea should slowly disappear by the time you drift off to sleep. If the mixture causes vomiting, you should not repeat the procedure at this time. This occurs only in *rare* cases. The gallbladder/liver flush stimulates and purges these organs. Women who have chronically suffered from gallstones, backaches, nausea, and more occasionally find small gallstone-like objects in the stool the following day. These objects are light green to dark green in color. They are very irregular in shape, gelatinous in texture, and vary in size from grape seeds to cherry pits. If you see a large number of these objects in the stool, the liver flush should be repeated in two weeks.

## YOUR STRUCTURAL/NEUROLOGICAL SYSTEM

Do you suffer from frequent headaches? Headaches have many causes and fall into several categories.

*Migraines* can be devastating and disrupting to women's lives. It is estimated that nearly thirty million Americans currently suffer from these intense headaches that often last from four hours to two days.[4] Symptoms include nausea, vomiting, seeing an aura, chills, distorted taste and smell, and sensitivity to light and movement.

*Cluster headaches* cluster over the forehead or eyes; one eye may have tearing and distorted vision, nausea, and sensitivity to light and movement. They occur suddenly and are extremely painful, happening typically twice a day, and are often triggered by anger and histamine reaction. To relieve cluster headaches, use ginger or feverfew capsules, gingko biloba, vitamin C, or alpha lipoic acid. Add essential fatty acids to your diet.

*Sinus headaches* involve congestion and inflammation of the sinus passages, a dull ache over the eyes, irritability, and sleeplessness. To relieve sinus headaches, use Xlear Nasal Wash or rosemary tea.

*Tension headaches* are caused by muscle contractions in the temples or back of the head, usually caused by stress or fatigue, and may last for hours or days. Many women describe this type of headache as feeling like their head is in a vise. To relieve tension or stress-related headaches, drink Yerba Mate Green Tea.

> *Dr. Janet's Recommendation:*
>
> Drink plenty of liquids, because muscles need fluids to contract and relax. Electrolyte drinks are very helpful. Penta Water provides excellent hydration.

*Hormonal headaches* are experienced by many women near their cycle or around menopause due to high or excessive estrogen levels. To relieve hormonal headaches, rub natural progesterone cream on your temples.

Structural/neurological problems may also cause muscle cramps and spasms. *Muscle cramps and spasms* are usually caused by vitamin or mineral deficiencies, as well as metabolic insufficiency of magnesium, potassium, calcium, iodine, trace minerals, and vitamins D, E, and $B_6$. In addition, other factors include a lack of adequate HCL in the stomach, allergies, high blood pressure medication, and poor circulation.

### GUIDELINES FOR GETTING RID OF HEADACHES

Follow these dietary guidelines:

- Avoid headache triggers such as alcohol, wine, beer, dairy foods, caffeine, sugar, chocolate, wheat, sulfites, nitrates, MSG, and pizza.
- A cup of black coffee can relieve a headache once it has begun.
- Have a green drink daily (Kyo-Green).
- Have a cup of green tea sweetened with stevia.
- Add nuts (almonds), dark leafy greens (for magnesium), and broccoli, pineapple, and cherries (for vitamin C).
- Eat turkey to boost serotonin levels.

Try these herbal and natural remedies:

- Nature's Secret Ultimate Cleanse to detoxify
- Feverfew and gingko biloba
- Magnesium
- GABA and B-complex to calm and relax
- Evening primrose oil
- Dr. Janet's Woman's Balance Formula (progesterone cream) for hormonal headaches
- Carlson's ACES
- Bromelain
- 5-HTP to calm stress
- DLPA for pain
- Aromatherapy, especially lavender oil

Make these lifestyle changes:

- Massage therapy
- Therapeutic baths: sea salt, baking soda, and lavender oil
- Chiropractic
- Deep breathing
- Exercise
- Laughter is the best medicine!
- Ice pack applied to the back of the neck; for nausea, place ice pack on the throat
- For tension headache, take a brisk walk and breathe deeply.
- Take time out to focus on relaxation each and every day.

## EVALUATE YOUR CARDIOVASCULAR SYSTEM

Did you check any of the symptoms for your cardiovascular system?

High blood pressure is a major health problem for American women. Middle-aged women have a 90 percent chance of developing

THE TEN ESSENTIAL BUILDING BLOCKS

high blood pressure.[5] It is often called *the silent killer* because many cases are undiagnosed.

*Symptoms of hypertension*

- Dizziness
- Swollen ankles
- Great fatigue
- Ringing in the ears
- Red streaks in your eyes
- Frequent headaches and irritability
- Depression
- Kidney malfunction
- Respiratory problems
- Chronic constipation
- Weight gain and fluid retention

High blood pressure goes hand in hand with *circulatory problems.* Varicose and spider veins, cold hands and feet are all connected to the health of the circulatory system. Symptoms include high cholesterol and triglyceride levels, ringing in the ears, leg cramps, swollen ankles, chronic headaches, poor memory, dizziness, and shortness of breath.

*Dr. Janet's Recommendation:*

If a parent or sibling had early heart disease, and if you are obese, a smoker, or have other risk factors, ask your doctor about getting a cardiac CT scan to assess your real risk.

If your blood pressure is continually 100/60 or below, you have low blood pressure. With it come fatigue, low energy, light-headedness when standing up, nervousness, allergies, and low immunity. The causes for low blood pressure include endocrine or nerve disorders, reaction to medications, electrolyte loss, weak adrenal function, and emotional stress.

The most commonly recognized symptom for cardiovascular problems is chest pain. *Chest pain should always be evaluated by your health-care provider.* Heart attack symptoms are different in women. If you experience any of the following symptoms, you should visit your doctor.

### Heart Attack Symptoms in Women

The following symptoms can occur up to a month before a heart attack happens:

- Unexplained shortness of breath, often without pain
- Unusual attacks of indigestion, accompanied by teeth, jaw, ear, and/or back pain
- Poor sleep patterns with accompanying anxiety
- Unexplained unusual fatigue

The following symptoms may indicate a heart attack is imminent:

- Extreme fatigue, weakness, and dizziness
- Shortness of breath with palpitations and cold sweats

### YOUR IMMUNE SYSTEM

Women who live in today's world are all susceptible to stress. Stress, when not managed and dealt with properly, can lower immunity. One sure sign of lowered immunity is chronic infections like colds or respiratory allergies. If you add antibiotic therapy into the mix, you are depressing immunity even more, opening the door to candida yeast infections.

Your immune system is a miraculous healing machine made up of microscopic cells. It attacks and destroys disease-causing invaders and abnormal or infected cells.

*Dr. Janet's Recommendation:*

If you suspect you are having a cardiac event, call 911 and consider the following natural emergency rescues from nature: one teaspoon of cayenne powder in water or cayenne tincture; chew an aspirin with water, which may help to reduce an arterial blockage.

THE TEN ESSENTIAL BUILDING BLOCKS

Your immune system is key to defending you from parasites, toxins, and bacteria. Furthermore, the immune system plays a significant role in helping prevent or reduce the effects of various diseases and much more. A compromised immune system can hinder your body's ability to guard against disease and toxins. It is vitally important for you to restore, strengthen, and balance your immune system. Your immune system requires the right raw materials to produce the internal medicines to safeguard you from illness. If you are experiencing any of the symptoms of low immunity, the following guidelines will support and strengthen your immunity.

## Supporting Your Immune System

Follow these guidelines to support your immune system for optimal health:

- Consume a diet as close to the "original garden" as possible with plenty of fresh fruits and vegetables, high-fiber foods, seafood, yogurt, and kefir.
- Add garlic and onions to your favorite dishes for added immune-boosting benefit.
- Avoid sugary foods (pies, cakes, etc.), which depress immunity.
- Eliminate fried foods, refined foods, and red meat.

Be aware that sugar consumption inhibits immune function, starting just thirty minutes after consumption and lasting more than five hours. One hundred grams of sugar in any form—honey, table sugar, fructose, or glucose—can reduce the ability of your immune system to engulf and destroy invaders. Women typically reach for sugar in times of stress or tension. This is especially detrimental to our balance, because it makes our bodies acidic and strips us of stabilizing B vitamins. Diseases that are known to be caused in part by excessive sugar consumption are hypoglycemia and diabetes.

## WOMEN AND OUR RESPIRATORY SYSTEM

If you have experienced any of the common symptoms of lowered respiratory function, the protocols included in later chapters of this book will be especially beneficial in terms of balancing your body.

In the case of asthma, there are many causes and triggers. Allergies to dairy and wheat are common triggers. In addition, animal dander, molds, chemically sprayed produce, and food additives can trigger asthma attacks. Many women are diagnosed with this potentially dangerous condition around the time of perimenopause and menopause because asthma is often linked to adrenal exhaustion. It is at midlife that a woman's adrenal reserves are at their lowest due to emotional stress, poor diet, or not enough sleep or exercise. Knowing what your trigger is will be the first step in finding relief.

## A WOMAN'S GENITOURINARY TRACT

If you have experienced any of the symptoms of urinary dysfunction or imbalance, such as frequent urination, inability to control your bladder, recurrent kidney or bladder infections, or kidney stones, a bladder and kidney detoxification protocol is in order. Avoid all bladder and kidney irritants, such as spinach, red meat, and excessive protein consumption. Drink eight to ten glasses of water each day. The following supplements will help to support your entire genitourinary tract health. To alkalize, have a green drink daily—Kyo-Green, liquid chlorophyll, or chlorella; drink marshmallow tea; take goldenseal-echinacea capsules, vitamin C (1,000 mg), and grapefruit seed extract capsules as natural antibiotics with anti-inflammatory effects.

Add bladder and kidney cleansers, such as cranberry capsules or cornsilk tea. Take protease (an enzyme from a plant source to help prevent kidney stones). Drink dandelion tea, and take probiotics, lactobacillus/acidophilus. Make sure to take a fiber supplement or consume enough fiber on a daily basis to further strengthen the urinary tract system and reduce the risk of stones. Bladder infections are painful. Inflammation of the bladder is usually associated with *E. coli* bacterium. Over 75 percent of American women have at least one urinary tract infection in a ten-year period.[6]

Other causes include staph, strep, overuse of antibiotics with resultant yeast infection, lack of adequate fluid intake, poor elimination, stress, and the tissue changes that occur with premenopausal/menopausal years.[7]

## YOUR EYES AND EARS

A woman's eyes are truly the windows to her soul. You can tell much about a woman's state of being just by looking into her eyes. Your eyes mirror your physical, mental, and emotional health. You will want to keep your eyes healthy, thereby preserving the most precious of your senses—your eyesight. Strengthen your eye health with natural supplements that support eye vessel health, including bilberry, alpha lipoic acid, lutein, and quercetin. Use antioxidants like eyebright, beta-carotene, zinc, taurine, vitamin E, and astaxanthin.

### TAKE GOOD CARE OF YOUR EYES

1. *Macular degeneration* (AMD) is often improved with targeted nutritional therapy, which must be consistent. If you are suffering with AMD, stop smoking immediately. Begin a walking program, and watch your diet. Eat healthy, especially dark, leafy greens, and lose any excess weight. Take lutein and zeaxanthin.

2. *Eye floaters* can also be improved by addressing liver health. Follow the gallbladder/liver flush suggestions given earlier in this chapter, and stay on liver nutritional support for at least three months to "see" noticeable improvement. The most important

supplements to include are milk thistle, triphala, and dandelion tea.

3. *Dark circles* under your eyes are often indicative of allergies, iron deficiency, and liver malfunction or sluggishness. Take triphala capsules to help detoxify the liver.

4. *Cataracts*: To avoid the development of cataracts, include glutathione, vitamin C, and cysteine.

5. *Night blindness*: Make sure you see your ophthalmologist on a regular basis. Add spinach to your diet, and supplement your diet with vitamin A, bilberry, ginkgo biloba, $CoQ_{10}$ (100 mg), and zinc (30 mg) daily.

6. *Dry eyes*: For dry eyes, take high omega-3 flax oil and four capsules of evening primrose oil daily. Ginkgo biloba and bilberry will help bring circulation to the eyes, as well as act as natural antihistamines. I personally love Similasan Eye Drops #1 to moisturize and soothe my eyes.

There are also many natural recommendations for the ear conditions that many people experience. Most ear problems are the result of an infection. The cause may be swimmer's ear, food allergy, ringing in the ear (tinnitus), or a cold- or flu-related secondary infection.

Earaches can be controlled and/or prevented by boosting your immune system. (See chapter three for supplements to support immunity.) You can fight ear infections with grapefruit seed extract, Xlear Nasal Wash, and echinacea extract. You may also drop 1 ounce of 70 percent isopropyl alcohol into your ear, tilt your head, and let it drain out after ten to sixty seconds. This will help to dry up moisture or water in the ear that could lead to infection. For pain associated with infection, make ear drops with warm olive oil and Kyolic Liquid garlic extract, or place a small cotton ball soaked in onion juice in your ear canal.

While dealing with an ear infection, eliminate all dairy foods and sugars from your diet, and drink plenty of water and chamomile tea.

Tinnitus, or ringing in the ear, may be caused by a chronic ear infection or wax buildup. It may also be the result of ototoxic medications like antibiotics and aspirin. TMJ (temporomandibular joint) disorder can also be involved. Exposure to loud music or physical trauma to the face or head can also play a role in its development. In addition, high cholesterol and triglyceride levels may cause tinnitus.

Avoid food triggers like chocolate, coffee, caffeine, and sodas, and eliminate dairy, wheat, corn, and fried, salty, and sugary foods.

## A WOMAN'S ENDOCRINE SYSTEM

A woman's endocrine system is by far the most delicate and most crucial when it comes to vibrant health, balance, and well-being. The extensive list of symptoms included in the Know Your Body Self-Assessment Screening should tell you that your endocrine system helps to regulate everything from energy flow (thyroid and adrenal glands) to inflammation to your monthly cycle.

Womanhood is a wonderful experience when a woman's system is in balance. The endocrine system is delicately tuned and can become imbalanced, causing discomfort and poor function. From puberty to premenopause to menopause to postmenopause, many women in today's stress-filled world are affected by significant imbalances and fluctuations in their endocrine system, which makes life difficult. Fibroids, headaches, PMS, endometriosis, depression, low sex drive, and infertility are all indicative of the need for endocrine balance. Finding and maintaining your hormonal balance is not easy in today's world. (See chapter nine for more helpful information.) In addition to extreme stress, today's environment contains estrogen mimics known as *xenobiotics* or *xenoestrogens*. Xenobiotics have a profound impact on hormone balance. Most of them are petrochemically based. Perfumes, pesticides, soaps, clothing, medicine, microchips, plastics, and medicines all have a petrochemical connection. In addition, growth-promoting hormones are injected into our food supply, particularly in beef and poultry products. This contributes to estrogen dominance in relationship to progesterone levels.

When you add in a high-stress lifestyle, which depletes your adrenal glands, you add in another huge player in the endocrine imbalance picture. A natural protocol for balancing your endocrine system complete with lifestyle therapy can help you rebalance your thyroid, adrenal, and reproductive hormone levels gently, thereby bringing harmony to your body and quality of life. (See chapter nine.) An endocrine hormone-balancing program is especially beneficial after periods of stress, trauma, a hysterectomy, childbirth, serious illness, or surgery.

## YOUR MIND—ACHIEVING EMOTIONAL BALANCE

Now that you are armed with physical health-balancing protocols, it is time to evaluate your current state of emotional health. We are emotional beings. Emotions often control every fiber of our being. To experience the full range of emotions—happiness, sadness, hate, love, excitement, boredom, empathy, and apathy—is to enjoy the passion of life itself. Without emotions we would be nothing more than robots. We could not enjoy the wonders of this world if we did not have emotions attached to what we hear, say, and see. If we never experienced sadness or boredom, how could we relate to or appreciate happiness, joy, or excitement? While no one likes to experience negative emotions, they can serve as catalysts for growth and pathways to a richer existence.

As women, all too often we grow up learning defense mechanisms that hide our true feelings, and we survive by becoming the image of what we believe is acceptable. This image robs us of true happiness. We begin to live lives that others have chosen for us, and we deny the beauty of who we really are. Emotions are powerful. Take heed, because they serve as teachers of what is important in our lives. If you ignore your emotional self, then you will pay a very heavy price. Emotions that are not dealt with can keep you from fulfilling your true divine destiny.

No matter what condition you are in, whether you are suffering from stress, fibromyalgia, panic attacks, muscle tension, lupus, chronic fatigue, or depression, remember one thing: it took many years and many life events to bring you to this current level of health. The good news is that even though you may feel defeated, the truth is, you do still have some level of health.

The very fact that you are reading this book indicates that you may be feeling overwhelmed by your life or your poor health. You will be surprised to see how much better you will feel just by understanding why you feel the way you do.

## YOUR EMOTIONS AND THE ILLNESS CONNECTION

Let's begin our look at a woman and her emotions by using the How Do You Become Ill? self-assessment review to analyze your current emotional balance.[8]

### How to Get Sick

- Blame other people for your problems.
- Do not express your feelings and views openly and honestly.
- Be resentful and hypercritical, especially toward yourself.
- If you are over-stressed and tired, ignore it and keep pushing yourself.
- Avoid deep, lasting, intimate relationships.
- Worry most, if not all, of the time.
- Follow everyone else's opinion and advice while seeing yourself as miserable and stuck.
- Don't have a sense of humor; life is no laughing matter.
- Do not make any life-enriching changes.

### How to Become Sicker

(If you are already sick)

- Dwell upon negative, fearful images.
- Be self-pitying, envious, and angry. Blame everyone

and everything for your illness.

-◈- Give up all activities that bring you a sense of purpose and fun.

-◈- Cut yourself off from other people.

-◈- Complain about your symptoms.

-◈- Don't take care of yourself, because what's the use?

-◈- Listen to conflicting medical opinions, and never follow through with any advice.

-◈- See your life as pointless.

## How to Stay Well or Get Better

-◈- Release all negative emotions, resentment, envy, fear, sadness, and anger. Express your feelings; don't hold on to them.

-◈- Do things that bring a sense of fulfillment, joy, and purpose and that validate your worth.

-◈- Pay close and loving attention to yourself by nourishing and encouraging yourself.

-◈- Love yourself, and love everyone else. Make loving a primary expression in your life.

-◈- Pray and give thanks to God continually.

-◈- Keep a sense of humor.

-◈- Accept yourself and everything in your life as an opportunity for growth and learning.

-◈- Be grateful.

-◈- Make a positive contribution to your community through some sort of work or service that you enjoy.

-◈- Try to heal any wounds from past relationships.

## DEALING WITH EMOTIONAL PAIN

According to Kevin Lane Turner in his book *A Journey to the Other Side of Life*, there are three sources or roots of emotional pain.[9] They are

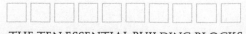

THE TEN ESSENTIAL BUILDING BLOCKS

wounding, unfulfilled emotional expectations, and the habits that are a result of the wounding and unfulfilled expectations. Let's dissect them.

## Roots of Emotional Pain

### Wounding

A wounding is a hurt that was inflicted upon you by someone that you loved or cared for. This wounding either betrayed you or violated you. A wounding could have been a major one-time event or a series of woundings throughout your life. The pain of a wounding, generally, has been with you a long time deep inside your core or heart.

### Unfulfilled expectations

This is when you look to a person, relationship, job, or project of some kind to work out a certain way. The problem begins when it does not turn out the way you planned or expected, and the disappointment drained you emotionally. This often appears after divorce or any relationship that ends. Many times we are guilty of placing demands, desires, emotional hopes, and dreams on those closest to us in order to feel loved and accepted. This really isn't fair. It only pressures those closest to you and results in them pulling away. Then comes the feeling of rejection, which adds another straw to the camel's back.

### Habits

Habits are the third source of emotional pain. Because of the wounding and unfulfilled emotional expectations, we acquire negative habits that hinder us from overcoming the pain that torments our heart. Emotional pain that is not dealt with affects the way we react on a daily basis. Emotional pain can cause habits that make us think, say, feel, and do things that are not really a reflection of our true selves; set us up for more pain; and make us feel guilty, weak, a bad person, and inferior.[10]

How do you heal and overcome the wounding and get back to your old self again? Volumes have been written on this topic. The self-help industry is booming.

It has been said that the power unleashed by your emotional self is far greater than the power of your body.[11] When you are depleted from wounding, anxiety, stress, or pain, your emotional self becomes so powerful that it can make you physically do, say, and think things that you normally would not. When you are replenished and balanced, your emotional self becomes an outlet for you to express love, happiness, and peace. So, how do you "get a grip" on years of wounding and depletion? The answer is simple: You must understand your feelings. You must learn how your emotional self works. To heal your emotional self is to learn to control your emotions. Now remember, emotions are powerful. You can't harness them, but you can learn to control your emotional response. This is done by forgiving the people or situations that have wounded you. This will release your heart, and you will be able to experience love and peace.

To bring balance and healing to your emotional self you must learn to change channels when your past hurt, anger, unforgiveness, trauma, or grief resurfaces. Choose to forgive, and then let it go. You must not dwell on the past. Do not relive it. Change the channel in your mind to forgiveness, or bitterness will set in. Remember, what you won't let go of won't let go of you. The Bible says that we should forgive seventy times seven, and that we will be shown the same amount of mercy that we have shown others. (See Matthew 18:22; Romans 11:31.)

You have the ability to forgive and let go. Again, it is a conscious choice. But do you have the desire? Life is too short. If you live a life of unconditional love, you will reap a life of freedom and abundance.

See the best in people. Repay evil with goodness and mercy. It is a small price to pay when you consider the reward of sound emotional health and a body that is free of disease.

THE TEN ESSENTIAL BUILDING BLOCKS

## DEPRESSION

Depression has risen to epidemic proportions in this country. According to an article in *USA Today*, a study published by the *Journal of the American Medical Association* showed that the percentage of Americans being treated for depression more than doubled during the ten-year period between 1987 and 1997, with the number of individuals receiving treatment increasing to 6.3 million.[12] Women seem to be more susceptible to depression than men,[13] maybe because women are thought of as being more *emotional*, or there may be a female reproductive hormone connection. At any rate, scientific studies are showing that by taking specific amino acids to restore the brain, depression can be alleviated.

Emotions play a part in this devastating condition, which leads to depletion. The underlying origins for depression are bottled-up anger or aggression turned inward, great loss and the inability to express grief, and negative emotional behavior often learned in childhood to control relationships. There may also be drug-induced depression, because prescription drugs create nutrient deficiencies. Amino acid deficiency occurs when there is prolonged and intense stress. This creates a biochemical imbalance with nutrient deficiencies.

Listed below are the ten warning signs of anger. If you can relate to any of the signs, anger could be playing a big part in your emotional and physical health.

### Ten Warning Signs of Anger

Place a check mark in the boxes that you recognize as areas where you need better balance.

- ☐ Overly critical
- ☐ Low self-esteem
- ☐ Divorced parents
- ☐ Inability to get close to people
- ☐ Overly controlling
- ☐ Blame others for mistakes

☐ Untrusting

☐ Confrontational

☐ Overreactions

☐ Indifference or nonsupport from parents

Forgiveness is the antidote for anger. It literally short-circuits a cascade of stress hormones that accelerate heart rate, shut down the immune system, and encourage blood clotting. Conversely, unforgiveness and holding on to anger increase your chance of a heart attack fivefold! They also increase your risk of cancer, high blood pressure, high cholesterol, and a host of chronic diseases.

Forgiveness is a decision you have to make. You must consciously choose to give up your feelings of unforgiveness and anger. Forgiving is not necessarily forgetting. It is unrealistic to think that you can forget about an injustice, hurt, or wound inflicted upon you by someone you love. You do have a memory, and the memory will always be with you. Forgiving is letting go of the anger and hurt attached to it and moving on with your life.

Forgiveness lowers blood pressure according to a study at Florida Hospital in Orlando, Florida. A group of hypertension patients took an eight-week forgiveness-training program, conducted by head researcher Dick Tibbits. The patients who took forgiveness training had lower blood pressure than the control group who did not. The most dramatic reductions in blood pressure occurred in people who began the program with a lot of anger issues.[14]

## RECOGNIZING DEPRESSION

A woman is considered depressed if she exhibits at least four of the symptoms listed below nearly every day for at least two weeks. Clinical depression is very different from emotions that are an integral part of the human experience, like sorrow, anger,

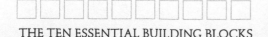

THE TEN ESSENTIAL BUILDING BLOCKS

fear, and guilt. According to the National Institute of Mental Health in 2001, chronic, mild depression affects roughly 3.3 million U.S. adults in a given year.[15]

- Fatigue and loss of energy
- Insomnia or increased sleep
- Feelings of worthlessness, self-reproach, or excessive or inappropriate guilt
- Loss of interest or pleasure in usual activities, or decrease in sexual drive
- Diminished ability to think or concentrate, or indecisiveness
- Recurrent thoughts of death or suicide, or suicide attempts
- Agitation or sluggishness in movement
- Poor appetite and significant weight loss or increased appetite and significant weight gain

## Overcoming depression

Many women have experienced "the blues" at some point in their lives. Maybe it was the baby blues following childbirth, or maybe the blues came after the death of a loved one, a failed relationship, job loss, or even the death of a beloved pet. These days, just reading the newspaper or listening to a news program can send us into a tailspin. But usually, with time our grief dissipates and our mood lightens, allowing us to go on with life.

But true depression is not a temporary condition. It is much more serious and cuts into our soul. It is a powerful affliction that can leave us totally debilitated, unable to deal with daily responsibilities, to maintain relationships, or to hold a job. It is a total body disease with far-reaching symptoms that damage our physical and emotional state.

Researchers have now discovered that several neurotransmitters or chemical messengers, including serotonin, dopamine, and norepinephrine, regulate our moods and keep us happy. Depressed women tend to have lower levels of serotonin, norepinephrine, and dopamine. This may explain the occurrence of endogenous depression, which comes from nowhere, seems to linger forever, and ruins the lives of many.

Depression tends to run in families, but a great deal of research has gone into looking for psychological or environmental causes. Unrelenting stress, anger, and hopelessness are often seen as precursors to depression. Nutritional deficiencies, thyroid disorders, allergies, chronic pain, and hormonal imbalances can also play a role.

There are natural solutions to the problem of depression. You must begin by eliminating three substances from your diet: alcohol, which is a depressant; caffeine, which can leave you physically and mentally drained; and sugar. After giving you a burst of energy, sugar causes a letdown, which will leave you tired and depressed. (See chapter eleven for my protocol for depression.)

## YOUR SPIRIT—ACHIEVING SPIRITUAL BALANCE

You will discover in this book that achieving balance in your life will require a commitment from you to seek balance in your physical life, your emotional life, and your spiritual life. If you deal with the physical issues in your life only, you will have overlooked the core or root of many of the physical distresses you are facing. Can you truly live a balanced life? I believe that you can, but you must have the willingness and desire to do so. You must do the work…you must find the balancing tools to bring you into proper balance in all areas of your life. It may be the most difficult task you have undertaken. Looking deep within yourself takes a lot of courage. That is where God comes in and holds you up as you go deep within. With His help, the process of achieving balance is accelerated. So prayer and a close relationship with your Creator are imperative. You will then experience life as God intended it to be, for you will be all that He created you to be.

The root of many of the physical ailments that cause imbalance in our lives lies deep within our hearts and emotions. The Bible tells us that "what comes out of the mouth gets its start in the heart" (Matt. 15:18,

THE TEN ESSENTIAL BUILDING BLOCKS

The Message). Another verse expands on that thought by saying, "As [a man] thinks in his heart, so is he" (Prov. 23:7, NKJV). James Allen, in his classic book *As a Man Thinketh*, states:

> Disease and health, like circumstances, are rooted in thought. Sickly thoughts will express themselves through a sickly body. Thoughts of fear have been known to kill a man as speedily as a bullet, and they are continually killing thousands of people just as surely though less rapidly. The people who live in fear of disease are the people who get it. Anxiety quickly demoralizes the whole body, and lays it open to the entrance of disease; while impure thoughts, even if not physically indulged, soon will shatter the nervous system.[16]

When it comes to your health, your thoughts are a key to balance. As you allow your thoughts to focus on your Creator, carefully monitoring your thoughts on a daily basis, you will move forward to emotional and spiritual balance, and, ultimately, to physical balance in your life.

Research has uncovered one of the greatest healing miracles of all time—spiritual balance in your life. More than three hundred studies confirm that people of faith are healthier than nonbelievers and less likely to die prematurely from any cause. Having faith can also speed recovery from physical and mental illness, surgery, and addiction.

According to Dale A. Matthews, MD, an associate professor of medicine at Georgetown University School of Medicine in Washington DC and author of *The Faith Factor*, the body responds positively to faith.[17] Blood pressure and pulse rate tend to be lower, oxygen consumption better, brain wave patterns slower, and immune function enhanced if you practice your faith regularly.[18]

Now you can see how important it is to concentrate your efforts to achieve balance in your relationship with your Creator—your faith in your God.

### BALANCING YOUR LIFE—BODY, MIND, AND SPIRIT

In the final pages of this first chapter, I am providing you with a tool I am calling The Achieving Balance Worksheet to help you begin to recognize the areas in your life where you need to set some goals for achieving balance. As you continue to read the remaining chapters of this book, refer back to this worksheet as you discover steps to take to bring balance to your life.

## THE ACHIEVING BALANCE WORKSHEET

Place numbers 1 through 6 on the lines below, putting 1 on the line where you feel your life is most balanced, and 6 on the line where you feel you are most out of balance:

_____ Work

_____ Play

_____ Friends

_____ Family

_____ Love

_____ Worship

*Is your life out of balance?*

1.  Where do you spend most of your time?

    _____

2.  Where do you spend too little time?

    _____

3.  In order to balance your life, what areas do you need to focus on?

    _____

4.  What action will you take to bring the main areas of your life into balance?

    _____

    _____

## Balancing My Body

What nutritional areas need to be brought into better balance in your life?

_____

_____

_____

How can exercise become a regular part of your daily life? It is crucial for physical and emotional well-being.

Form of exercise? _____

How many times a week? _____

For how long? _____

Aerobic exercise? _____

Weight training? _____

To recover from stress, I will:

_____ Watch my sugar intake.

_____ Limit or eliminate caffeine.

_____ Eliminate alcohol.

_____ Eat whole, live foods and minimally processed foods.

_____ Take dietary supplements that boost my body and brain function daily.

## Balancing My Emotions

It is important to forgive and release all feelings of hurt and wounding. Check off the following list of relationships that have been affecting your emotional health. Then list the emotion that is connected to that relationship.

| Relation | Emotion |
|----------|---------|
| Mother | _____ |
| Father | _____ |
| Brother | _____ |
| Sister | _____ |

| Relation | Emotion |
|----------|---------|
| Wife | _____ |
| Husband | _____ |
| Boss | _____ |
| Co-worker | _____ |
| Child | _____ |

In each case where you checked a relationship problem, a conscious effort must be made on your part to address the hurt, to forgive or ask for forgiveness, and finally, to heal the relationship. Then, let go once and for all. Only then can you move on.

Relax…you deserve it! Take time daily to relax. Make the following relaxation techniques a part of your daily life. You must give yourself time to unwind, or you will remain tense or irritable. During relaxation, the body repairs, de-stresses, and rebuilds.

To relax, I will:

    _____    Have a weekly massage.

    _____    Take a warm aromatherapy bath.

    _____    Relax with a good book.

    _____    Take a relaxing walk.

    _____    Pray or meditate.

    _____    Practice deep breathing or the MANTLE technique every night before bed. (See chapter ten.)

    _____    Listen to soothing music.

## BALANCING MY SPIRIT

To balance my spirit, I will:

    _____    Love unconditionally.

    _____    Forgive.

    _____    Use faith to banish my fear.

    _____    Pray.

    _____    Read only uplifting materials.

*Out with the old—in with the new.*

Get control of your life! Eliminate from your life things that are not working, and focus on the things that are working. This will help eliminate frustration and stress. It is liberating!

*Things that are working:*

| Personal Life | Business Life |
| --- | --- |
| | |
| | |
| | |
| | |

*Things that are **not** working:*

| Personal Life | Business Life |
| --- | --- |
| | |
| | |
| | |
| | |

## CONCLUSION

Now that you have completed your initial body, mind, and spirit self-evaluation, you are now armed with the knowledge of the areas in your life where you need to experience greater balance. Now it's time to move forward and discover the "Ten Essential Building Blocks" for achieving balance in your life. Each of these building blocks will be vitally important as you begin your journey to a body balanced by nature—physically, emotionally, and spiritually.

Do not be overwhelmed with all of the recommendations. Just set your own pace. Remember that this is *your* journey to balanced health. It is not a race. You have already won just by taking the first step.

# CHAPTER 2

# NUTRITIONAL BALANCE

It would be impossible to minimize the role that good nutrition plays in your overall health and body balance. The nutrients that you consume each day, and virtually every bite of food you take, give you energy to do your work and to empower your body with vibrant health.

Your body uses nutrition to build, maintain, and repair your tissues. Nutrients empower your cells to relay messages back and forth to conduct essential chemical reactions that enable you to think, see, hear, smell, taste, move, breathe, and eliminate waste. Is good nutrition crucial to body balance and vibrant health? You bet it is! But getting reliable information about nutrition can be a challenge. In this chapter I will focus on the important role nutrition plays in supporting a woman's health. Good nutrition is the foundation of healthy cells; it provides antiaging benefits, aids the production of energy, and protects from disease. Many women neglect to nourish their bodies with life-giving nutrients because they are so involved with caring for others that they fail to devote their attention to healthy dietary practices. This chapter will educate you on what foods are best for your personal health and well-being. Once you apply these recommendations, you will be able to make informed dietary choices that will in turn help you to look and feel younger and, of course, be healthier.

As women, we share the same physical makeup, but each of us is as individual as our thumbprint when it comes to our specific nutritional

needs. Many factors combine to determine your individual nutritional needs, including:

- The amount of stress you experience and how you manage it
- How your hectic lifestyle depletes your nutritional storehouse
- What your dietary habits are
- Whether you are overly acidic or overly alkaline

## ACID OR ALKALINE?

In its natural state, a woman's body is slightly alkaline. Alkalinity must be maintained for your survival. All parts of your body work in synergy to prevent your body from becoming overly acidic or overly alkaline. In childhood, most of us are naturally alkaline. This is also true into our teens and early adulthood. By the fourth decade of life, most women become overly acidic. This is because of our exposures to stress, poor food selections, and environmental toxins, all which take a toll. Our *natural buffer systems,* which are normally in place in our earlier years, become less efficient over time. This causes a shift to a more acidic internal environment.

Before I discuss balancing your system with fresh, whole-food nutrition, you must determine if you are overly acidic, which makes you susceptible to many ailments—including headaches, chronic illnesses, colds and flu, digestive problems, urinary tract infections, and chronic fatigue.

Women with a healthy acid/alkaline balance are blessed with mental clarity, fast recovery from illness and injury, vitality, and energy. Once you determine whether you are acidic or alkaline, you will be able to eat right for your body type. The good news is that if you fall into the overly acidic category, you can bring your system into a more alkaline state by eating foods that will turn the condition around fairly quickly.

Check the appropriate boxes in each list:

## ACIDITY SCREENING

☐    Do you have a history of arthritis, gout, lung disease, or frequent bladder infections?

☐    Are you susceptible to environmental allergies, heartburn, food allergies, and skin eruptions?

☐    Do you have frequent colds, flu, bronchitis, or sinusitis?

☐    Are you physically and mentally tired after an hour of deskwork?

☐    Do you feel most healthy when you are on a vegetarian diet?

☐    Do you have trouble tolerating white flour, citrus fruits, and vinegar?

☐    Does drinking coffee, alcohol, or colas make you feel bad?

☐    Do you feel less than your best when you eat red meat or sweet desserts?

## ALKALINITY SCREENING

☐    Do you have lots of energy in the midst of intense conditions?

☐    Do you feel bright and energized after a steak dinner?

☐    Do you need only a few hours of sleep each night?

☐    Are you always on the go and full of energy?

☐    Do you gravitate toward high-stress activities?

☐    Do you have no problem digesting a wide variety of foods?

☐    Do you feel tired after a low-protein, high-carbohydrate meal?

☐   Are you strong with a large frame and big bones?

☐   Do you rarely get a cold or the flu, and are you free of allergies?

Based upon your answers, you will now be able to recognize the foods that are contributing to your poor quality of life and the ones that will balance your pH and bring you back to vibrancy.

These foods should make up your daily eating plan. Eat as close to the original garden as possible. Make sure that you are working on alkalinizing your body, especially if you fit the overly acidic profile. Your body will feel the difference in no time.

*Dr. Janet's Recommendation:*

If it does not rot or sprout, do without.

For a nutritional intake that will keep your body alkalinized, make the following foods the centerpiece of your daily regimen.

- *Legumes*: baked beans, kidney beans, lima beans, soybeans, tofu, chickpeas, black beans
- *Grains*: brown rice, barley, oats, rye, millet, quinoa, hominy grits, buckwheat
- *Poultry/eggs*: free-range chicken, duck, turkey, egg yolk, whole eggs
- *Meat*: substitute fish, shellfish, poultry, eggs, and tofu for red meat and pork
- *Condiments*: hot peppers, garlic, canned olives, flax meal, kelp
- *Sweeteners*: blackstrap molasses, honey, brown rice or maple syrup
- *Vegetables*: pumpkin, sweet peppers, spinach, carrots, squash, asparagus, turnip, cabbage, broccoli, sweet potato, onion, peas, celery, corn, lettuce, mushrooms, brussels sprouts

- *Unsweetened fruits*: figs, papaya, persimmon, dates, cantaloupes, melon
- *Nuts and seeds*: walnuts, almonds, flaxseed, hazelnuts, pecans, poppy seeds, pumpkinseeds, sesame seeds, sunflower seeds
- *Beverages*: mineral water, distilled water, herbal or green tea; substitute soy or rice "milk" for cow's milk. Coffee and tea are acidic even if decaffeinated.[1]

In the following chart, I have listed highly acidic, moderately acidic, and less acidic foods so that you can make the necessary changes to your daily diet in order to bring your pH back to normal. Remember, when your body is in a healthy, balanced state, it is slightly alkaline with a pH reading between 7.35 and 7.45. Anything below 7.0 is considered acidic. You should purchase a pH test paper kit from your drug store so that you can test your alkalinity. Use it to test your saliva and your urine to get a baseline. Then monitor your progress as you implement the recommended dietary changes.

### FOODS AND THEIR ACIDITY

| Highly Acidic | Moderately Acidic | Less Acidic | |
|---|---|---|---|
| Tomato juice | Beer | Mineral water | Scallops |
| Apple juice | Bananas | Coffee | Catfish |
| Orange juice | Mangoes | Distilled water | Sardines |
| Wine | Pears | Milk | Crab |
| Lime juice | Peaches | Figs | Shrimp |
| Lemon juice | Cherries | Avocado | Molasses |
| Ginger ale | String beans | Melon | Cocoa |
| Apple cider | Eggplant | Dates | Honey |
| Prune juice | Tomatoes | Papaya | Dutch cocoa |
| Cranberries | Sausage | Peppers | Syrup |
| Cucumbers | Cottage cheese | Spinach | White bread |
| Yogurt | | Butter | Wheat |
| Strawberries | | Broccoli | Rice |

## Foods and Their Acidity

| Highly Acidic | Moderately Acidic | Less Acidic | |
|---|---|---|---|
| Blackberries | | Garlic | Barley |
| Blueberries | | Onion | Oats |
| Raisins | | Peas | Rye |
| Pineapple | | Celery | Quinoa |
| Jellies | | Most cheeses | Amaranth |
| Grapefruit | | Corn | Hominy |
| Apples | | Mushrooms | Most beans |
| Plums | | Cauliflower | Lima beans |
| Oranges | | White potatoes | Soybeans |
| Limes | | Asparagus | Walnuts |
| Lemons | | Lettuce | Almonds |
| Vinegar | | Chicken | Pumpkinseeds |
| Pickles | | Duck | Sesame seeds |
| Mayonnaise | | Egg yolk | Flax |
| | | | Sunflower seeds |

If you are overly acidic, you will feel better if you consume more carbohydrates in your daily diet. If you are a high alkaline producer, you will feel better if your diet contains more proteins.

## LEAN MEAT, POULTRY, AND FISH

If you are a high alkaline producer, you need to consume several 4-ounce portions of lean meat, poultry, and fish each day to feel your best. Try to make the most of your choices from skinless poultry and fish. If you tend to be overly acidic, most of your protein should come from a combination of whole grains and legumes, with an occasional serving of salmon or skinless poultry. Always limit your red meat or pork to only two servings each month. I recommend fish and poultry for both metabolic types because they are lower in unsaturated unhealthy fat. Most importantly, they contain a full spectrum of essential amino acids needed to build protein and are great sources of vitamins E, D, and A. Poultry sources include turkey, duck, goose, and free-range chicken. Fish include trout, perch, and bass, which provide omega-3 fatty acids that fight inflammation and reduce your chance of stroke. Saltwater fish include tuna, flounder, red snapper, swordfish, and salmon, which are also rich in omega-3 oils.

## VEGETABLES

I consider *vegetables* to be *body builders*. They are an excellent way to receive your daily supply of nutrients. Most vegetables register low on the acidity scale. They are a great choice for women on both sides of the pH scale. Vegetables deliver the most nutritional value when they are eaten raw. But many women complain of stomach and intestinal bloat when consuming raw veggies. This can be alleviated by simply adding a digestive enzyme supplement from a plant source as mentioned earlier in chapter one. When choosing vegetables for your diet, look for as many colors as possible, because each color offers you even more nutritional benefit. For example, green vegetables like spinach and kale help you cope with stress. Carrots and yams can help improve your resistance to allergies and help manage PMS and excessive menstrual bleeding. Onions, garlic, mushrooms, and ginger may slow or even prevent tumor growth. Be adventurous and try vegetables that you have never eaten before, and remember that when you do, health benefits are certain!

## FRUITS

*Fruits* are nature's way of smiling. They have been referred to as "nature's candy." They are wonderful system cleansers. They have a naturally high water and sugar content that speeds up your metabolism to release wastes quickly.

Fresh fruit has an alkalizing effect on the body and is extremely high in vitamins and nutrition. The good news here is that natural fruit sugars are easily transformed into quick, nonfattening energy that speeds up your metabolism. This is true for fresh fruits only! Fruits that are cooked are changed from alkalinizing to acid forming in your body.

Fresh fruits should be eaten before noon for best energy conversion and cleansing benefits.

Fruits offer you a wonderful source of potassium, calcium, magnesium, and vitamin A. Vitamin A is an important player in the prevention of many types of cancer and safeguards against cardiovascular events such as stroke and heart attack. It is also very important for clear vision and strong immunity. Potassium helps to regulate your body's fluid balance. Women with low potassium levels often have low stamina and fatigue easily. If you fall into the overly acidic category, I recommend that you avoid citrus fruits and choose less acidic ones such as bananas, melon, and mangoes. You should try to have three to five servings per day.

> ### Dr. Janet's Recommendation
>
> If you are overly acidic, or if you suffer from candida yeast overgrowth, hypoglycemia, chronic fatigue, or high triglycerides, limit your servings of fruits to one or two servings daily.

## JUICING

By now, I am sure you have heard about juicing and how beneficial it is for your body. Thanks to the "Juice Man," millions of Americans have heard about juicing and the incredible amount of nourishment it gives our body. Why is juicing so health promoting? Because juices extracted from fresh raw fruits and vegetables furnish all the cells in the body with the elements they need in the manner in which they can be easily assimilated.

Fruit juices are the cleansers of our bodies, and vegetable juices are the builders and regenerators of our systems. Vegetable juices contain all the minerals, salts, amino acids, enzymes, and vitamins that the human body requires. This is why both fruit and vegetable juices are so important in a body-balancing immune-system makeover.

Another benefit of adding juices to your body-balancing plan is that juices are digested and assimilated within ten to fifteen minutes after consumption, and they are used almost completely by the body to nourish and regenerate the cells, tissues, glands, and organs. The end result is very positive because of the minimal effort needed by the digestive system.

One of the most important things to remember about juicing is to always drink your juices fresh daily. That is when they are at their peak as far as nutritional value. Also, fresh juices spoil quickly, so it is better to make fresh juice daily. In addition, if you are ill or have a history of digestive difficulty, be sure to dilute your juice with water in a 50/50 mix. This way you will prevent any bloating, gas, or discomfort you may experience from taking all of this liquid nutrition into your body.

As a general rule of thumb, 1 pint daily is the least amount needed that will show any result. When I was regaining my health, I drank 2 to 3 pints daily. I have included some of the same juice recipes that I have personally used and ones that I have recommended to my clients for various sub-health conditions. Drink fruit juices at different times of the day than vegetable juices in order to prevent stomach upset.[2]

Fruit and vegetable juices are beneficial for many conditions and ailments that result from imbalance in your body. Try the combination of fruits and vegetables recommended below for various ailments and conditions. The fruits and vegetable used have been shown to aid your body in finding relief and healing from each condition.

### JUICING FOR TOTAL BODY BALANCE

It is important to wash the fruits and vegetables in ten drops of grapefruit seed extract in a basin of water before juicing. Grapefruit seed extract is a disinfectant that kills yeasts, mold, and fungi. Be sure to scrub the fruits and vegetables with a brush to help remove any pesticide residue.

(Note: These are separate formulas for therapeutic juice drinks for each condition.)

*Arthritis—choose one or more of these juices:*

- Celery
- Grapefruit
- Carrot and spinach
- Carrot and celery

*Anemia—choose one or more of these juices:*
- ↬ Carrot, celery, parsley, and spinach
- ↬ Carrot and spinach
- ↬ Carrot, beet, and celery

*Bladder trouble—choose one or more of these juices:*
- ↬ Carrot and spinach
- ↬ Carrot, beet, and cucumber
- ↬ Carrot, celery, and parsley

*Bronchitis—choose one or more of these juices:*
- ↬ Carrot and spinach
- ↬ Carrot and dandelion
- ↬ Carrot, beet, and cucumber

*Colds—choose one or more of these juices:*
- ↬ Carrot, beet, and cucumber
- ↬ Carrot, celery, and radish
- ↬ Carrot and spinach

*Constipation—choose one or more of these juices:*
- ↬ Spinach
- ↬ Carrot
- ↬ Carrot and spinach

*Fatigue—choose one or more of these juices:*
- ↬ Carrot
- ↬ Carrot and spinach
- ↬ Carrot, beet, and cucumber

*Fever—choose one or more of these juices:*
- ↬ Grapefruit
- ↬ Lemon
- ↬ Orange

*Gallbladder and gallstones—choose one or more of these juices:*
- ↬ Carrot, beet, and cucumber
- ↬ Carrot and spinach
- ↬ Carrot, celery, and parsley

*Headaches—choose one or more of these juices:*
- Carrot and spinach
- Carrot, celery, parsley, and spinach
- Carrot, lettuce, and spinach

*Insomnia—choose one or more of these juices:*
- Carrot and spinach
- Carrot and celery
- Carrot, beet, and cucumber

*Liver problems—choose one or more of these juices:*
- Carrot
- Carrot, beet, and cucumber
- Carrot and spinach

*Menopausal symptoms—choose one or more of these juices:*
- Carrot and spinach
- Carrot, beet, lettuce, and turnip

*Nervous tension—choose one or more of these juices:*
- Carrot and spinach
- Carrot and celery
- Carrot, beet, and cucumber

*Sciatica—choose one or more of these juices:*
- Carrot and spinach
- Carrot, spinach, turnip, and watercress

*Sinus trouble—choose one or more of these juices:*
- Carrot
- Carrot and spinach
- Carrot, beet, and cucumber

*Ulcers—choose one or more of these juices:*
- Cabbage
- Carrot and spinach
- Carrot, beet, and cucumber[3]

## FATS

Fatty acids provide protection to your body. They provide protection to your bones and joints; they support the function and development of your adrenal glands, your inner ear, your eyes, and your reproductive tract. They help to reduce inflammation. They are essential to energy production, they help to regulate hormone and metabolic functions vital to circulatory health, and they are major components of all cell membranes. The following chart will give you the essential fatty acids (EFAs) to include in your diet.

### ESSENTIAL FATTY ACIDS (EFAs)
- Linolenic acid
- Gamma-linolenic acid (GLA)
- Arachidonic acid

## GRAINS

A healthy diet contains three or more servings of whole grains each day. If you are a high alkaline producer, you should limit your intake of grains and choose to get your fiber from fruits and vegetables.

Whole grains like oats, rye, millet, amaranth, quinoa, barley, whole-grain breads and pasta, and buckwheat provide fiber, protein, carbohydrates, fats, a wealth of minerals, B-complex vitamins, and other vitamins and lignans, which help with many reproductive problems.

Whole grains can help lower your total cholesterol by binding to it and helping to eliminate it from your body. Millet, in particular, is helpful for alkalizing the stomach and is acceptable for women who have wheat allergies and candida yeast overgrowth. Quinoa is gluten free. Oats are excellent fiber grains that help to lower cholesterol and promote regularity. Buckwheat is a *non-wheat* grain. Barley is a low-gluten flour with a sweet malty taste.

Amaranth is an ancient Aztec grain-like seed that contains high-quality protein. It is compatible with a diet to control candida yeast overgrowth. Whole grains also serve us well as women because the fiber they contain binds to the estrogen your body is trying to discard and makes sure that it is eliminated. In addition, the complex carbohydrates found in whole grains stabilize levels of serotonin, which in turn helps you calm down and relax.

## LEGUMES

If you are overly acidic, you now know that you must reduce your consumption of animal protein. Wonderful sources of legumes include lima beans, pinto beans, garbanzo beans, navy beans, lentils, peas, and soybeans. All are great sources of fiber and complex carbohydrates. When you add in whole grains, you create the same balance of amino acids that is equivalent to protein. This is great news for the overly acidic woman as she tries to change her internal pH more in favor of alkalinity. Legumes are rich sources of B vitamins. If you combine them with whole grains and leafy vegetables, you are insuring that your body is receiving inflammation-fighting essential fatty acids.

Tofu, soybeans, and soy milk are sources of isoflavones, which are weak estrogens (plant based) that can be a blessing during perimenopause, because they take the edge off of the estrogen dominance that so often occurs. During actual menopause, isoflavones can actually boost the amount of estrogen your body is still producing. Studies on isoflavones have shown that it helps to lower cholesterol and is a heart-healthy food. Research has linked a high intake of soybean-based foods to the lower incidence of breast cancer in women. When combined with whole grains, tofu yields a complete protein. It provides dairy richness without the fat or cholesterol.

## NUTS AND SEEDS

Nuts and seeds are little storehouses of nutrition complete with omega-3 and omega-6 fatty acids, B-complex vitamins, and a plethora of minerals. The really great thing about them is that they help keep your skin

supple and moist. This includes vaginal and bladder mucosa during your perimenopausal/menopausal transition and beyond!

Almonds, pecans, walnuts, sunflower seeds, pumpkinseeds, sesame seeds, and flaxseeds all offer you a bounty of benefits. I sprinkle them on salads and whole-grain cereals. They make a great garnish for fruit salads, too! Try to have ¼ cup of seeds or nuts several times a week.

## WATER

Many women suffer from aches and pains, constipation, skin eruptions, and fatigue. You may find it hard to believe, but a lack of water is often behind some of these common complaints. Our society consumes coffee by the gallons and soft drinks and iced tea by the liter. Plain old water for some people is just plain boring. Many clients informed me on their first visit that they did not drink water, but they made sure they drank enough liquids each day. I asked them to tell me what liquids they were referring to. You guessed it—iced tea, coffee, concentrated juices, and soft drinks! I often saw clients who ingested large quantities of vitamin supplements every day with a glass of iced tea or soda. No wonder these women were having problems.

Water makes up 65 to 75 percent of our body. It is second only to oxygen for our survival. Water helps to flush wastes and toxins, regulates body temperature, and acts as a shock absorber for joints, bones, and muscles. It cleanses the body inside and out. It transports nutrients, proteins, vitamins, minerals, and sugars for assimilation. When you drink enough water, your body works at its peak. Many of my clients who had a problem with water retention, edema, and bloating were simply not drinking enough water. Once they did, these symptoms improved. If you are trying to lose weight, you should know that when you drink enough water, hunger is curtailed.

To maintain the proper function of your system, you must start drinking good, clean water every day. The recommended amount is six to eight glasses per day. If this seems like a lot to you, just start slow. Add a slice of fresh lemon, and you will get even more of a cleansing benefit.

In addition, a hint of flavor from a lemon makes it easier to drink more. This always worked for my clients who believed that they could never increase their water intake. Now I see these women out and about with a bottle of water in their hand. This only proves that they now know how much better they feel just by drinking enough water. They are so convinced that they carry it with them.

Now that you understand the health benefits of drinking water, the next question is this: what kind of water should you be drinking? This is a good question since most of our tap water is chlorinated, fluoridated, or treated to the point of being an irritant to the system. Many toxic chemicals have found their way into the groundwater, adding more pollutants to our water supply. This growing concern about water purity has led to the huge bottled water industry. Stores today have whole aisles dedicated to bottled water.

Let's go over the different types of water to clear up any confusion. First, we have mineral water, which most often comes from a natural spring with naturally occurring minerals and a taste that varies from one spring to the next. Naturally occurring minerals found in mineral water help to aid digestion and bowel function. Europeans have long known the benefits of bottled mineral water.

Next, we have distilled water. You may know someone who believes that drinking distilled water is the only way to go. I disagree. While it is true that distilled water is probably the purest water available, it is demineralized. I believe that drinking demineralized water on a long-term basis is not ideal. I believe that you need the minerals that naturally occur in water. While distilled water is a good cleanser and detoxifier, I don't believe that it is a good builder, because it is devoid of minerals. If you are on a detoxifying program or on chemotherapy, distilled water is excellent to remove debris and toxins. After you are finished with detox or chemotherapy, then return to drinking a good mineral or spring water to insure proper mineral activity.

Sparkling water is another choice that comes from natural carbonation in underground springs. Most brands of sparkling water are

artificially boosted in carbonation by $CO_2$ to maintain a longer fizz. Many people enjoy sparkling water after dinner to aid digestion.

A bottled water that is being called "the next generation" water is Penta, a purified drinking water that is the cleanest bottled water known. Drink Penta water for ultimate hydration. Penta's eleven-hour, thirteen-step purification process removes impurities found in even the healthiest of mountain spring waters. Studies show that Penta water leaves the stomach quickly, improves physical performance, increases muscle efficiency, and dissolves the main ingredient in kidney stones faster. Penta's clean, crisp taste and the youthful, more energetic feel you have after being effectively hydrated will make you a firm believer in ultra hydration.[4]

These days you may see water filters you may attach to your kitchen sink faucet that remove impurities as water flows out of the tap. You may also have noticed water pitchers that contain filters to purify the water as you fill the pitcher. I feel that these two inventions are quite necessary to help improve the quality of the water we consume. Both options, I feel, are acceptable for health building. Whatever type of water you choose, the most important thing to remember is that you must pay conscious attention to getting your quota of water every day. Thirst is not a reliable signal that your body needs water. You can easily lose a quart or more of water during activity before you even feel thirsty. Also, remember that caffeine and alcohol are diuretics. They increase your body's need for water. If you consume caffeine or alcohol, please make sure you drink enough water to compensate. Ideally, caffeine and alcohol do not belong in a health-building program.

### Are You Drinking Enough Water?

*Dehydration signs:*

- Unexplained headaches, dizziness, and fatigue
- Unusually dry skin
- Loss of appetite along with constipation
- Weight gain with swollen hands and feet

- Dull back pain not relieved by rest
- Worsening of MVP (mitral valve prolapse) symptoms
- Unexplained irritability, impotence, restlessness, and difficulty sleeping

Do a simple urine test: if your urine color is dark yellow, start drinking more water. You will know that you are adequately hydrated when your urine becomes a pale straw color.

## WATER WISDOM

To help educate you on water filtration, here is a chart that will make you an authority on the subject.

*Filter Type: Distillation*

- **Cost:** $800–$4,500 for whole house system
  $100–$1,000 countertop model
  $600–$1,100 freestanding unit
- **How They Work:** Boils water, leaving contaminant behind. This purified water vapor is then condensed to a liquid.
- **What They Reduce:** Chromium, lead, nitrates, sulfate, giardia, arsenic, cadmium.

*Filter Type: Reverse Osmosis (known as "RO" Water)*

- **Cost:** $150–$200 countertop model
  $600–$1,500 under the counter
- **How They Work:** Pressurized water is forced through a purifying membrane that eliminates contaminants; purified water then goes to a holding tank.
- **What They Reduce:** Radium, chromium, iron, cadmium, color, chlorine, lead, radium, giardia, sulfate.

*Filter Type: Carbon Filtration*
- ◈ **Cost:** $25–$30 faucet model
    $350–up under the counter
- ◈ **How They Work:** Water is passed through a carbon or charcoal block, which traps contaminants. Filters must be replaced periodically.
- ◈ **What They Reduce:** Chlorine, odors, chemicals, pesticides, bad taste.

*Filter Type: Water Softener*
- ◈ **Cost:** $1,000–$3,500
- ◈ **How They Work:** Uses sodium (rock salt) to "soften" the water.
- ◈ **What They Reduce:** Calcium, radium, and iron.[5]

## DIETARY HEALTH ROBBERS

I would be remiss if I did not list what I feel to be the biggest dietary health robbers of our time. The following foods have little or no place in a body-balancing program because they offer little if any nutritional benefit and may even leach many valuable nutrients from your body.

*Caffeine*

Caffeine stimulates the release of stress hormones, which will increase any feelings of nervousness or anxiety you may have as well as steal valuable nutrients from the rest of your body that are needed to feed your stressed nervous system. In addition, caffeine triggers panic and anxiety symptoms, reduces absorption of iron and calcium, worsens breast pain, increases the frequency of hot flashes, and acts as a diuretic, speeding the elimination of valuable minerals and vitamins you need. It increases acid production in the stomach and raises blood levels of cholesterol and triglycerides. I recommend that you slowly wean yourself off caffeine by reducing your daily intake until you are *caffeine free*. There are wonderful decaffeinated teas and beverages to choose from. If you love chocolate, simply switch to carob. Roasted dandelion tea is a good coffee substitute, or you may try Pero, Postum, or Caffix.

*Dairy*

Many women who complain of fatigue, bloating, depression, intestinal gas, nasal congestion, postnasal drip, and wheezing may suffer from a food sensitivity. Most often the culprit is dairy. Dairy products are one of the primary sources of food allergies in the standard American diet. Delayed reactions such as mood swings, dizziness, headaches, and joint pain can occur. When you add the fact that hormones and pesticides are used in livestock feed, cow's milk is not a healthy choice. Another important consideration is lactose, which is the predominant sugar in milk and cannot be digested by many women. The good news is that there are wonderful dairy substitutes that are full of calcium and are easy to assimilate. Try soy milk, rice milk, or almond milk; try sorbet or other frozen desserts make from rice milk. Make smoothies with soy milk, rice milk, or almond milk. Try soy, almond, or rice cheese. Your body will quickly let you know that you have made a healthier choice. Watch all of your allergic symptoms disappear in about seven to fourteen days.

*Salt*

Salt is one of your body's most important minerals along with potassium. It helps regulate your cell's water balance. Women with low blood pressure or low adrenal function (hypoadrenia) can benefit greatly by adding ⅛ teaspoon of sea salt to an 8-ounce glass of spring water every morning to help increase blood volume and adrenal function. Most women, however, consume too much salt. It is very easy to do these days due in part to our fast-paced lives where we dine out frequently or buy frozen dinners to use in a *pinch*. We may habitually oversalt our foods or add some to the dishes we prepare, then salt them again before we take the first bite.

Salt can cause fluid retention and breast tenderness, and it can increase your risk of hypertension (high blood pressure) and heart disease. I recommend you try some of my favorite salt substitutes. Try using fresh herbs to season your foods; they enhance the flavors. For example, garlic and lemon are wonderful. Sprinkle Spike or Mrs. Dash on your favorite foods. In no time you will make them a permanent addition to your diet!

### Margarine

Margarine contains trans fats, which are bad for your heart. I want to encourage you to stop using margarine and replace it with olive oil for cooking, canola oil when baking, Benecol or Spectrum Spread on baked goods, or maybe a low-sugar fruit spread. On baked or mashed potatoes, why not try salsa or a little light olive oil and black pepper?

To reduce your intake of saturated fats, which are found in dairy, red meat, and eggs, substitute them with the following, as I do: Use applesauce instead of oil when baking deserts. Use a canola- or safflower-based mayonnaise, and replace corn chips and potato chips with baked, low-salt chips. Have turkey burgers or garden burgers or a veggie dog at your next backyard cookout.

### Sugar

When it comes to dietary acid, excessive sugar intake can rob you of your health. Regular sugar intake is known to play a negative part in a host of our most common diseases, including hypoglycemia, heart disease, high cholesterol, obesity, nearsightedness, eczema, psoriasis, dermatitis, gout, yeast infections, and tooth decay. Sugar is addictive, affecting the brain first by offering you a false energy lift that lets you down lower than when you started.

In times of stress, depression, and anxiety, women often reach for sugar. This is especially detrimental to your brain and body function. In addition, excessive sugar consumption has been shown to suppress your body's immune response. If you are consuming too much sugar on a daily basis, you may be setting yourself up for low blood sugar. Many women who suffer from anxiety and depression also have to deal with hypoglycemia. Notice how the symptoms of anxiety are identical to the profile of a hypoglycemic individual.

### Sugar Sabotage

- Rapid pulse
- Crying spells
- Heart palpitations
- Weakness
- Cold sweats
- Irritability
- Fatigue
- Nightmares
- Twitching
- Poor concentration

If these symptoms are familiar to you, you must focus on eating more fiber and protein foods at each meal and on cutting back on simple sugars. It is very important that you have a protein snack between meals. This will keep your blood sugar levels stable all day long. It is true that limiting or even eliminating sugar will not be easy, but in order to rebuild your brain and body, sugar consumption must be curtailed. The following dietary supplements will help you make the adjustment.

### Dietary Supplements That Support Blood Sugar Levels

- Chromium picolinate
- B complex
- Vitamin C
- Pantothenic acid
- Adrenal gland supplement
- Calcium and magnesium
- A protein shake each morning
- Stevia extract as a sugar-balancing herbal sweetener
- Fiber in your diet (brown rice, for example)

It is wise to balance your blood sugar now because low blood sugar can predispose you to developing diabetes later in life. Diabetes occurs when all of the sugar and carbohydrates that a person consumes are not used properly. The pancreas no longer produces insulin, creating high blood sugar. This can be very dangerous. According to the U.S. Department of Health and Human Services, more than 20 million people suffer from diabetes in this country.[6] Diabetes can lead to heart and kidney disease, stroke, blindness, hypertension, and even death.

## Is Your Sugar Consumption Affecting Your Health?

Take this short quiz to see if your sugar consumption may not only be affecting your level of health now, but later on as well.

Yes    No

____  ____    Do you have a family history of diabetes?

____  ____    Do you crave sweets at certain times of the day?

____  ____    When under stress, do you crave sweets?

____  ____    Do you consume ice cream, chocolate, pies, cakes, and candy more than twice a week?

____  ____    Do you feel weak and shaky if your meal is delayed?

____  ____    Do you feel tense, uptight, and nervous at certain times during the day?

____  ____    Do you crave sodas or other sweetened soft drinks?

____  ____    Do you pay attention to low-fat foods while ignoring the higher sugar content typically found in them?

A study at the University of Alabama showed that people suffering from depression had fewer symptoms when sugar was removed from their diets.[7] In addition, excessive sugar consumption leads to:

- High cholesterol and triglycerides leading to risk of atherosclerosis
- Excessive emotional swings and food cravings, especially before menstruation
- Tooth decay and gum loss
- Even small blood sugar fluctuations disturb a person's sense of well-being. Large fluctuations caused by consuming too much sugar cause feelings of depression, anxiety, mood swings, fatigue, and even aggressive behavior.

By combining low-glycemic foods, like fiber foods, along with exercise, amino acid supplementation, and nutritional supplements that help balance your blood sugar, you will optimize your brain biochemistry.

You'll be interested to know that people who consume too much simple sugars and who are under constant stress are typically low in chromium. I have often seen my clients experience a heightened sense of well-being after following a healthy eating plan and taking chromium picolinate. I have also found that chromium seems to increase energy levels. I believe this is because of the blood-sugar balancing effect on the body. The energy peaks and valleys disappear and are replaced with an even, sustained energy. In

> *Dr. Janet's Recommendation:*
>
> No sugar? But how? Chromium will help you as you wean yourself off simple sugars that have been robbing you of your health.

addition to chromium, I recommend pantothenic acid, which is a B vitamin that helps the body handle stress. This vitamin does wonders for your adrenal glands that are so often zapped by caffeine, sugar, lack of sleep, and stress. (See the next chapter for more information on these supplements.)

Pantothenic acid and chromium picolinate will help you make the lifestyle changes you need to experience a balanced mind and body. Instead of sugar, I personally use stevia extract to sweeten my teas or anything that requires sweetening. You will find it to be a wonderful blessing that is noncaloric and is safe for diabetics and hypoglycemics.

## PERSONALITY PERILS OF SUGAR

*Mental and emotional signs of too much sugar:*

- Chronic or frequent bouts of depression with manic depressive tendencies
- Difficulty concentrating, forgetfulness, or absentmindedness
- Lack of motivation, loss of enthusiasm for plans and projects
- Increasing independence, inconsistent thoughts and actions
- Moody personality changes with emotional outbursts
- Irritability, mood swings

*Brain and body symptoms associated with excess sugar consumption:*

- Anxiety and panic attacks
- Bulimia
- Candidiasis, chronic fatigue syndrome
- Diabetes or hypoglycemia
- Food addiction with loss of B vitamins and minerals
- Obesity
- Menopausal mood swings and unusual low energy[8]

## WHY ELIMINATE ARTIFICIAL SWEETENERS?

America has jumped on the artificial sweetener bandwagon. This is because of our obsession and preoccupation with our weight. This seems like a simple answer for those trying to watch their sugar calories. Did you know that one of the components of aspartame is methanol? Methanol is also known as wood alcohol. Why would you even consider putting that into your body? Methanol is considered toxic even in small amounts. In addition, toxic levels of methanol have been associated with brain swelling, inflammation of the heart muscle and the pancreas, and even blindness! I recommend that you read *Aspartame: Is It Safe?* by H. J. Roberts.[9] In it you will read about reports of convulsions, memory loss, mood swings, headaches, nausea, and more. Aspartame, which is made synthetically, has also been implicated in fetal brain damage.[10]

> Japan has banned the use of aspartame (NutraSweet). Stevia is the #1 sweetening agent in Japan.

Pregnant and lactating women, or very young or allergy-prone children, should avoid aspartame.

And then we have the next generation of artificial sweeteners—Splenda. Here's the scoop: Splenda, also known as sucralose, or chlorinated sucrose, is four hundred to eight hundred times sweeter than sugar. It is seen as a chemical in your body and not as a carbohydrate. It has no effect on insulin secretion or carbohydrate metabolism.

Here is what you should know: Research from the Japanese Food Sanitation Council reveals that up to 40 percent of this sweetener is absorbed and may concentrate in the liver, kidneys, and gastrointestinal tract. In animal tests, sucralose is linked to a 40 percent shrinkage of the thymus gland, enlarged liver and kidneys, decreased red blood cell count, aborted pregnancy, and diarrhea.[11]

There are natural whole-food sweeteners that can satisfy your occasional sweet tooth without risk to your health.

### Natural Whole-Food Sweeteners

- **Honey**—twice as sweet as sugar. Avoid if you are diabetic or have candida or low blood sugar. It contains vitamins and enzymes.
- **Rice syrup**—40 percent as sweet as sugar, made from rice and water.
- **Sucarat**—natural sweetener made from sugar cane juice; a concentrated sweetener that should be used with caution if you have blood sugar imbalance.
- **Stevia**—herb from South America can be used in beverages, baking, and cooking. It is safe for persons with blood sugar imbalances and/or candida and diabetes. Stevia comes in two forms: liquid extract or white powered extract. Stevia is my personal favorite!
- **Fructose**—twice as sweet as sugar. It is derived from fruit and is not allowed if you have candida.

*A sweet secret*

Scientific research has revealed that stevia effectively regulates blood sugar. This is of vital importance for people who have either high or low blood sugar. In some South American countries stevia is sold as a helpful aid to people with diabetes and hypoglycemia.

Other studies have demonstrated that stevia lowers elevated blood pressure but does not seem to affect normal blood pressure. Stevia inhibits the growth and reproduction of some bacteria and other infectious organisms, including the bacteria that cause tooth decay and gum disease. This may help explain why users of stevia-enhanced products report a lower incidence of cold and flu. It has exceptional qualities when used as a mouthwash and toothpaste, and there have been reports of significant improvement in gum disease following a regular practice of using stevia.[12]

Stevia is a wonderful aid in weight loss and weight management because it contains no calories. Research indicates that it significantly increases glucose tolerance and inhibits glucose absorption. People who ingest stevia daily often report a decrease in their desire for sweets and fatty foods.

Other benefits of adding whole-leaf stevia to the daily diet are that it improves digestion and gastrointestinal function, it soothes upset stomachs, and it helps speed recovery from minor illnesses. An interesting but undocumented claim made by many users is that drinking stevia tea or stevia-enhanced teas or placing stevia leaves in the mouth reduces desire for tobacco and alcoholic beverages.

> *Dr. Janet's Recommendation:*
>
> Stevia can be used as part of a healthy diet for anyone with blood sugar problems since it does not elevate blood sugar levels. It has a zero glycemic index rating.

Stevia is currently in use as a healthful, no-calorie sweetener in South America, China, Taiwan, Thailand, Korea, Malaysia, Indonesia, and Japan. Stevia in these countries enjoys a 41 percent share of the commercial sugar-substitute market.

## CANDIDA

A stress-related condition that results in a seriously compromised immune response is candida (candidiasis). Because we are talking about nutritional guidelines for balanced living in this chapter, I want to address the issue of candida and help you recognize and deal with this health robber through a sound, healthy, nutritional plan.[13]

Candida is a fungal infection of the mucous membranes that affects the mouth, genitals, gastrointestinal tract, skin, and bloodstream. It causes symptoms such as constipation, muscle and joint pain, clogged sinuses, vaginitis, kidney and bladder infections, memory loss, mood swings, adrenal problems, low blood sugar, thyroid problems, hormonal imbalances, severe itching, prostatitis, diarrhea and colitis, and as many as a hundred more symptoms.

Candida albicans normally lives harmlessly in the gastrointestinal tracts and genitourinary areas of your body. However, if your immune response is reduced, as mine was, from repeated courses of antibiotics, a high-sugar diet, and lack of rest and relaxation, candida then multiplies too quickly, causing major health problems. The yeast colonies establish a foothold and flourish throughout the body, releasing toxins into the bloodstream.

To see if candida overgrowth could be contributing to your body imbalance, complete the following candida questionnaire, which was developed by Dr. William Crook, author of the wonderful book *The Yeast Connection*.[14] Fill out and score the questionnaire to see if the possibility of yeast overgrowth is a contributing factor to your lack of nutritional balance.

## Is Candida Robbing My Nutritional Balance?

*Section A: History*
Scoring for Section A: At the end of each question is the score for a yes answer.

| Score | Question |
| --- | --- |
| _____ | 1. Have you taken tetracycline or other antibiotics for acne one month or longer? (35) |
| _____ | 2. Have you at any time in your life taken broad-spectrum antibiotics or other antibacterial medication for respiratory, urinary, or other infections for two months or longer, or in shorter courses, four or more times in a one-year period? (35) |
| _____ | 3. Have you taken a broad-spectrum antibiotic drug, even in a single dose? (6) |
| _____ | 4. Have you at any time in your life been bothered by persistent prostatitis, vaginitis, or other problems affecting your reproductive organs? (25) |

_____    5.  Are you bothered by memory or concentrations problems? Do you sometimes feel spaced out? (20)

_____    6   Do you feel "sick all over," yet in spite of visits to many physicians, the causes haven't been found? (20)

            7.  Have you been pregnant:

_____        Two or more times? (5)

_____        One time? (3)

            8.  Have you taken birth control pills:

_____        For more than two years? (15)

_____        For six months to two years? (8)

            9.  Have you taken steroids orally, by injections, or inhalation:

_____        For more than two weeks? (15)

_____        For two weeks or less? (6)

            10. Does exposure to perfumes, insecticides, fabric shop odors, and other chemicals provoke:

_____        Moderate to severe symptoms? (20)

_____        Mild symptoms? (5)

_____    11. Does tobacco smoke really bother you? (10)

_____    12. Are your symptoms worse on damp, muggy days or in moldy places? (20)

_____    13. Have you had athlete's foot, ringworm, "jock itch," or other chronic fungus infections of the skin or nails? (10)

_____        Have such infections been severe or persistent? (20)

_____        Mild to moderate? (10)

_____    14. Do you crave sugar? (10)

_____        **TOTAL SCORE Section A**

*Section B. Major Symptoms*

These symptoms are often present in persons with yeast-connected health challenges:

Scoring system for Section B:

- Occasional or mild: 3 points
- Frequent and/or moderately severe: 6 points
- Severe and/or disabling: 9 points

| Score | Question |
|-------|----------|
| _____ | 1.  Fatigue or lethargy |
| _____ | 2.  Feeling of being "drained |
| _____ | 3.  Depression or manic depression |
| _____ | 4.  Numbness, burning, or tingling |
| _____ | 5.  Headaches |
| _____ | 6.  Muscle aches |
| _____ | 7.  Muscle weakness or paralysis |
| _____ | 8.  Pain and/or swelling in joints |
| _____ | 9.  Abdominal pain |
| _____ | 10.  Bloating, belching, or intestinal gas |
| _____ | 11.  Constipation and/or diarrhea |
| _____ | 12.  Troublesome vaginal burning, itching, or discharge |
| _____ | 13.  Prostatitis |
| _____ | 14.  Impotence |
| _____ | 15.  Loss of sexual desire or feeling |
| _____ | 16.  Endometriosis |
| _____ | 17.  Cramps and/or other menstrual irregularities |
| _____ | 18.  Premenstrual tension |
| _____ | 19.  Attacks of anxiety or crying |
| _____ | 20.  Hypothyroidism |

| | 21. Cold hands or feet, low body temperature |
|---|---|
| _____ | |
| _____ | 22. Shaking or irritable when hungry |
| _____ | 23. Cystitis or interstitial cystitis |
| _____ | **TOTAL SCORE SECTION B** |

*Section C: Additional yeast-related symptoms*

Scoring system for Section C:
- Occasional or mild: 1 point
- Frequent and/or moderately severe: 2 points
- Severe and/or disabling: 3 points

| Score | Question |
|---|---|
| _____ | 1. Drowsiness, including inappropriate drowsiness |
| _____ | 2. Irritability |
| _____ | 3. Incoordination |
| _____ | 4. Frequent mood swings |
| _____ | 5. Insomnia |
| _____ | 6. Dizziness or loss of balance |
| _____ | 7. Pressure above ears; feeling of head swelling |
| _____ | 8. Sinus problems, tenderness of cheekbones, or forehead |
| _____ | 9. Tendency to bruise easily |
| _____ | 10. Eczema; itching eyes |
| _____ | 11. Psoriasis |
| _____ | 12. Chronic hives |
| _____ | 13. Indigestion or heartburn |
| _____ | 14. Sensitivity to milk, wheat, corn, or other common foods |
| _____ | 15. Mucus in stools |
| _____ | 16. Rectal itching |
| _____ | 17. Dry mouth or throat |

_____  18. Mouth rashes, including "white tongue"

_____  19. Bad breath

_____  20. Foot, hair, or body odor not relieved by washing

_____  21. Nasal itching

_____  22. Nasal congestion or postnasal drip

_____  23. Sore throat

_____  24. Laryngitis, loss of voice

_____  25. Cough or recurrent bronchitis

_____  26. Pain or tightness in chest

_____  27. Wheezing or shortness of breath

_____  28. Urinary frequency or urgency

_____  29. Burning on urination

_____  30. Spots in front of eyes or erratic vision

_____  31. Burning or tearing eyes

_____  32. Recurrent infections or fluid in ears

_____  33. Ear pain or deafness

_____  **TOTAL SCORE SECTION C**

_____  **SECTION A**

_____  **SECTION B**

_____  **GRAND TOTAL SCORE**

How did you score? Women with a score over 180 and men with a score over 140 almost certainly have yeast-connected health problems. Women with a score over 120 and men and a score over 90 probably have yeast-connected health problems. Yeast-connected health problems are possibly present in women with scores over 60 and in men with scores over 40. With scores less than 60 in women and less than 40 in men, yeasts are less apt to be the cause of your health problems or lack of nutritional balance.

The plan of attack for overcoming the problems associated with candida is as follows:

1.  Kill the yeast through diet change and supplement therapy. I will give you guidelines for both in this chapter. Avoid antibiotics unless absolutely necessary. There are natural antibiotic alternatives.
2.  Detoxify the body to cleanse the dead yeast from the body.
3.  Use enzyme therapy to strengthen the digestive system in order to assimilate nutrients. Strengthen the liver and kidneys. Replant healthy bowel flora with friendly bacteria.
4.  Rebuild immunity. Follow my ninety-day immune system makeover.[15]

### *The candida diet*

The classic candida diet permits dense protein foods, such as chicken and fish, and as many vegetables as you can eat. Some people can use whole grains, while others cannot. Caffeine and alcohol should be avoided, as should foods made from flour: breads, pastas, tortillas, cakes, cookies, and so forth. Eliminate all sugar and all foods containing sugar. Read food labels carefully, as thousands of packaged foods contain sucrose, dextrose, glucose, fructose, corn syrup, maple syrup, honey, molasses, barley malt, and rice syrup. If sweetening is required, use stevia. Avoid foods that contain vinegar (mustard, mayonnaise, etc.), fermented foods (cheese, sauerkraut, soy sauce, etc.), and processed meats, especially hot dogs, sausages, bacon, and so on. Try to drink only filtered or bottled water, as tap water contains chlorine, which will further reduce the body's populations of friendly flora.

If you are a strict vegetarian, it is difficult to obtain enough complete protein without overloading on grains and beans. Eating a wide variety of vegetables at the same time can help counter this problem, as can supplements like spirulina and chlorella. Books with recipes for the candida diet can be invaluable.

## Foods You Can Eat Freely

- All fresh vegetables (except carrots and beets) and vegetable juices
- All fish (except scavengers and shellfish). Deep-sea white fish and salmon are particularly good.
- Stevia as a sweetener
- Free-range meats, ideally chicken and turkey
- Eggs
- Purified water
- Lemons, limes, cranberries, and Granny Smith apples Grapefruit and kiwi (after 20–60 days) Well-cooked grains: millet, buckwheat, amaranth, quinoa—*no wheat!*
- Pasta made from the above grains
- Essential fatty acids (Ultimate Oil and olive oil)
- Beans, grits, raw almonds, and seeds
- Pau de Arco tea

## Foods to Avoid

- Sugars: sucrose, fructose, maltose, lactose, glucose, mannitol, sorbitol, maple syrup, sugar, brown sugar, raw sugar, date sugar, corn syrup, and honey
- Aspartame and NutraSweet
- Yeast-containing foods, breads, and pastries
- Alcohol, soda, coffee, and fermented beverages (like cider)
- Cheese and sour milk products (sour cream and buttermilk)
- All nuts (except raw almonds)
- Mayonnaise, mustard, and ketchup
- Fruit (except ones mentioned above)
- Mushrooms (remember, yeast is a fungus)[16]

While the candida diet is rigid, it is necessary. As you begin to get yeast under control, you may be able to increase the levels of grains you eat and to add some fruits. If you do, be careful to monitor the way you feel and, at the first sign of recurring discomforts, return to the strict diet and begin using four capsules of Candex per day until the discomforts are once again under control. While some people say that after using Candex they have been able to reintroduce wider varieties of foods without incident, others report a rapid recurrence of discomforts when they do this.

With candida, you are battling digestive and intestinal problems, so probiotics are a must. These gastrointestinal defenders are crucial in keeping your immune defenses in good working order. These defenders known as *probiotics* consist mainly of lactobacillus acidophilus and lactobacillus bifidus. They produce volatile fatty acids that provide metabolic energy. In addition, they help you digest food and amino acids, produce certain vitamins, and, most importantly, make your lower intestine mildly acidic, which inhibits the growth of bad bacteria such as *E. coli*, which has caused serious illnesses in recent years.

Probiotic supplementation is absolutely essential in your fight against candida or any fungal infection because of the antifungal properties that these defenders possess. According to Drs. James and Phyllis Balch in their best-selling book *Prescription for Nutritional Healing*, the flora in a healthy colon should consist of at least 85 percent lactobacilli and 15 percent coliform bacteria.[17] The typical colon bacteria count today is the reverse, which has resulted in gas, bloating, intestinal and systemic toxicity, constipation, and malabsorption of nutrients, making it a perfect environment for the overgrowth of candida. By adding probiotics, that is, lactobacillus acidophilus and lactobacillus bifidus supplements, to your system, you will return your intestinal flora to a healthier balance and eliminate all of the problems of intestinal flora imbalance mentioned.

If you are on antibiotic therapy, it is vitally important that you supplement your digestive tract with probiotics or *good bacteria* because antibiotic use destroys your healthy bowel flora along with the harmful bacteria. Both L. acidophilus and L. bifidus promote proper digestion, help to normalize bowel function, and prevent gas and candida overgrowth. This in turn keeps immunity high.

Store your probiotic formula in a cool dry place. Some brands of probiotics require refrigeration. I personally prefer and use Bio-K and Kyo-Dophilus from Wakunaga of America. Kyo-Dophilus is milk free and remains viable and stable even at high temperature. It contains 1.5 billion live cells per capsule, is suitable for all ages, and contains L. acidophilus, B. bifidum, and B. longum in a vegetable starch complex. In addition, it is free of preservatives, sugar, sodium, yeast, gluten, artificial colors and flavors, and, as mentioned before, milk.

As a dietary supplement, take one capsule with a meal twice daily. Children under four should take one-half capsule with a meal twice daily. If the child cannot swallow the capsule, simply open it and sprinkle in juice or on food.

This is a wonderful formula for optimally balanced intestinal health. Probiotics: they are a good thing!

Dealing with your body imbalance through nutritional and natural guidelines will set you on the path to total body balance. In the next chapter we will see how natural herbal supplements and vitamins can partner with your nutritional plan to give you a woman's body, balanced by nature.

## Dr. Janet's Protocol for Colitis

### Natural Support for Colitis/IBS

- Heal intestinal lining with L-glutamine, MSM, chamomile tea, or slippery elm.
- Try antispasmodics in ginger/peppermint tea or a warm ginger compress to the abdomen.
- Calm nervous tension with valerian root, 5-HTP, or L-theanine.
- Support immunity with Lane Labs Nature's Lining, which helps to rebuild gastric tissue, or Chlorophyll Liquid (3 tsp. daily in water before meals).
- Have a green drink daily such as Kyo-Green.
- Use quercetin to reduce histamine reactions.

Use the following natural protocol to deal with any problems with constipation you may be experiencing.

### Dr. Janet's Protocol for Constipation

**NATURAL SUPPORT FOR CONSTIPATION:**

- Prevent constipation with probiotics—Primadophilus or Kyo-Dophilus.
- Normalize digestion with plant enzymes from Enzymedica with each meal.
- Add fiber to your diet with Benefiber or Fiber One cereal.
- Try natural laxatives like triphala, senna, or cascara sagrada.
- Quick cleanse your colon with vitamin C (3,000–5,000 mg) and bioflavonoids over a two-hour period, or use Colon Cleanse.
- Detoxify the entire body using Nature's Secret Ultimate Cleanse.

W omen of today are faced with challenges that their mothers and grandmothers never had to face. Many women raise children, take care of the home, run a home-based business, and manage the family's finances while being expected to be a perfect size six, to be active in the community and church, and to fill the role of family nutritionist, providing well-balanced, healthy meals, safe from pesticides, herbicides, radiation, and injected antibiotics and hormones. Quite a tall order, wouldn't you say?

That is why I wholeheartedly recommend dietary supplements to fill in any nutritional gaps that may be in our daily diet. As women, we often overlook our own nutritional requirements, leaving us depleted and underinsured nutrient-wise. In addition, illness, age, and extreme diet practices may put you in a spot where you cannot get all of the nutrients you need from food alone. Expecting busy women to make sure they consume enough calcium each day is not realistic, so the simple answer is to take a calcium supplement.

In this chapter I want to help you understand your daily supplemental needs for consistently vibrant health. Supplementing with the correct amounts of the right nutrients will enhance the function of the immune system, reproductive system, digestive system, and circulatory system. The right nutrient foundational protocol can help prevent disease as well as chase away fatigue, anxiety, headaches, and depression.

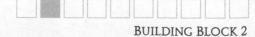

Again, my goal is to educate and arm you with all of the tools necessary to prevent illness and to strengthen and fortify your body. Experts agree that one of the best ways to safeguard your health is to eat only the healthiest foods you can find. Plenty of fresh fruits, vegetables, and whole grains, along with low-fat dairy, are the general recommendations. This is because of all of the *phytochemicals*, or vitamins, minerals, and fiber, that are naturally occurring in healthy foods and that are health protectors for your body.

Because of the enormous stress most women face today from work, family, and the pressures of life in general, most experts now agree that a multivitamin/mineral supplement makes perfect sense. A good vitamin supplement can fill, and close, nutritional gaps left by poor dietary habits. Evidence suggests that vitamins may increase our "health span," which means active years that are free from chronic illness.

> The only women not experiencing stress are buried in the graveyard.

When choosing a multivitamin, look for "USP" on the label. This means that the product has been formulated to dissolve 75 percent after one hour in body fluids. In addition, look for iron as ferrous fumarate or ferrous sulfate, because they are the most absorbable forms. For best absorption, take your multivitamin with meals and not on an empty stomach; otherwise you may experience nausea. Another important tip is to make sure that you take your multivitamin with a meal that contains a little fat. The fat-soluble vitamins A, D, and E need a little fat to get inside your system and go to work.

The outdated theory of mainstream medicine that holds that you can get all of the vitamins and minerals you need from your diet is slowly going by the wayside. More and more physicians are realizing that although our grandparents probably did receive all the nutrition they required from their foods, it is simply not the case in our generation. Mineral-depleted soils and chemical agribusiness farming and marketing methods do not guarantee that you will get anywhere near the ideal nutritional value from the foods you buy at the supermarket.

Maybe you have heard someone say, "Taking vitamins results only in expensive urine." The truth is, all substances are eventually excreted, but as your vitamins go on their way through your bloodstream, they build your health and enhance your life. Keeping your body blanketed with the full spectrum of vitamins and minerals is likened to having an insurance policy that will help to insure you against physical decline and degenerative disease.

*Dr. Janet's Recommendation:*
Brittle nails? Try biotin.[1]

## AN OVERVIEW OF VITAMINS AND HOW THEY WORK

Now, let's get you educated on vitamins and how they work together to strengthen and support your body.

### How Do Vitamins Work?

- **Vitamin C**: Builds collagen and maintains healthy gum, teeth, and blood vessels.
  *Sources*: grapefruit, oranges, strawberries, spinach, cabbage, melons, and tomatoes.
- **Vitamin D**: Aids calcium absorption and growth of bones and teeth.
  *Sources*: sunlight, salmon, tuna, eggs, milk, and butter.
- **Vitamin E**: Protects cells from damage.
  *Sources*: apples, peanuts, spinach, blackberries, wheat germ, nut and vegetable oils, and mangoes.
- **Vitamin K**: Improves blood clotting.
  *Sources*: eggs, carrots, avocados, tomatoes, parsley, cabbage, spinach, broccoli, and brussels sprouts.
- **Vitamin B$_1$, thiamine:** An antioxidant; enhances circulation, assists in the production

of hydrochloric acid, assists in blood formation, energizes, and promotes growth and learning capacity.

Sources: egg yolks, fish, wheat germ, oatmeal, peanuts, and poultry.

**Vitamin B$_2$, riboflavin:** Aids red blood cell formation.

*Sources*: cheese, milk, egg yolks, spinach, mushrooms, and broccoli.

**Vitamin B$_3$, niacin, niacinamide, nicotinic acid:** Promotes healthy skin and good circulation.

*Sources*: carrots, wheat germ, brewer's yeast, cheese, peanuts, and milk.

**Vitamin B$_5$ (pantothenic acid):** Antistress vitamin; plays a role in the production of abnormal hormones.

*Sources*: eggs, royal jelly, brewer's yeast, liver, and mushrooms.

**Vitamin B$_6$, pyridoxine:** Promotes cancer immunity and prevents arteriosclerosis by inhibiting homocysteine.

*Sources*: brewer's yeast, walnuts, eggs, spinach, peas, chicken, and bananas.

**Vitamin B$_{12}$, cyanocobalamin:** Prevents anemia and helps the utilization of iron.

*Sources*: seafood, dairy, eggs, brewer's yeast, and milk.

**Coenzyme Q$_{10}$, ubiquinone (CoQ$_{10}$):** A powerful antioxidant, important for the production of energy in every cell of the body.

*Sources*: salmon, sardines, mackerel, peanuts, spinach, and beef.

- **Biotin:** Aids in the metabolism of carbohydrates, fats, and proteins; aids in fatty acid production; and promotes healthy skin and nails.
  *Sources*: soybeans, whole grains, brewer's yeast, meat, milk, poultry, and cooked egg yolks.
- **Folic acid**: Needed for energy production and the formation of red blood cells.
  *Sources*: chicken, tuna, milk, liver, brown rice, salmon, wheat germ, and dates.
- **Choline**: Helpful for disorders of the nervous system and needed for the proper transmission of nerve impulses from the brain through the central nervous system. Without it, brain function and memory are impaired.
  *Sources*: soybeans, egg yolks, meat, and lecithin.

## MINERALS

A good multivitamin also contains minerals. Vitamins and minerals work together in synergy to boost and support our body's systems. Every living cell depends on minerals for proper function and structure. The balance of your body depends upon proper levels and ratios of different minerals. Minerals are crucial for proper nerve function, regulation of muscle tone, formation of blood and bone, and composition of body fluids. The entire cardiovascular system relies heavily on proper mineral balance.

> "The more I learn about nutritional supplements, the more I discover nutritional components that can help nearly everyone. In fact, I consider prescribing and individualizing of programs of vita-nutrients to be one of the two pillars of nutritional medicine."[2]
> —DR. ROBERT ATKINS

## How Do Minerals Work?

- **Calcium**: Promotes strong bones, teeth, muscle and nerve function, and blood clotting.
  *Sources:* salmon, sardines, yogurt, milk, cheese, broccoli, green beans, almonds, and turnip greens.
- **Chloride**: Aids digestion and works with sodium to maintain fluid balance.
  *Sources*: salted foods.
- **Chromium**: Assists with proper carbohydrate metabolism.
  *Sources*: broccoli, orange and grapefruit juice, brown sugar, cheese, and brewer's yeast.
- **Copper**: Helps with blood cell and connective tissue formation.
  *Sources*: oysters and shellfish, cocoa, cherries, mushrooms, gelatin, eggs, fish, and legumes.
- **Fluoride**: Strengthens tooth enamel.
  Sources: fish, tea, and fluoridated water.
- **Iodine**: Maintains proper thyroid function.
  Sources: iodized salt, shrimp, lobster, shrimp, oysters, spinach, and milk.
- **Manganese**: Aids calcium, phosphorus, and magnesium metabolism; provides support for healthy bones.
  Sources: mustard greens, kale, raspberries, pineapple, and collard greens.
- **Boron**: Needed in trace amounts; 2–3 mg needed by the elderly for proper calcium absorption.
  Sources: grapes, grains, apples, carrots, and leafy vegetables.
- **Zinc**: Sharpens taste and smell; a deficiency may result in taste and smell loss. It is essential for

prostate gland function and for proper reproductive organ growth. It may help curb acne because it can aid in the regulation of oil glands. It is wonderful for the immune system and aids in wound healing. In addition, it is required for proper collagen formation and protein synthesis. Zinc protects the liver from chemical assaults and is essential for proper bone formation.

Sources: mushrooms, egg yolks, sardines, whole grains, pumpkinseeds, sunflower seeds, and liver.

- **Phosphorus**: Found in most foods; most Americans have plenty in their systems due to the high rate of carbonated soft drink consumption. It is important for tooth and bone formation, kidney function, cell growth, and the contraction of the heart muscle.

  Sources: soft drinks (soda), pumpkinseeds, sunflower seeds, dairy products, eggs, fish, dried fruit, nuts, salmon, poultry, corn, and whole grains.

- **Iron**: Used in the production and oxygenation of red blood cells. It is essential for a healthy immune system.

  Sources: liver, meats, poultry, eggs, fish, almonds, avocados, blackstrap molasses, brewer's yeast, prunes, pumpkins, raisins, beets, peaches, and pears.

- **Germanium**: Carries oxygen to the cells, which in turn boosts immunity.

  Sources: mushrooms, garlic, and onions.

- **Magnesium**: Necessary to prevent the calcification of soft tissue. It helps prevent muscle tightness, dizziness, PMS, and high blood pressure, and it aids in the formation of bone.

  Sources: dairy products, meats, fish, nuts, molasses, brewer's yeast, avocados, and bananas.

- **Molybdenum**: Promotes normal cell function.
  Sources: dark leafy greens, peas, beans, and cereal.
- **Potassium**: Helps maintain regular heart rhythm. It is important for nervous system function.
  Sources: bananas, apricots, fish, dairy, garlic, nuts, yams, and wheat bran.
- **Selenium**: A vital antioxidant that inhibits the oxidation of blood fats (lipids); it protects the immune system from free-radical damage.
  Sources: brown rice, salmon, broccoli, brewer's yeast, dairy products, garlic, and liver.
- **Sulfur**: Disinfects the blood and protects against radiation; needed for the synthesis of collagen. It is a skin nutrient.
  Sources: garlic, wheat germ, onions, soybeans, eggs, fish, and brussels sprouts.

You may use the following chart as your guideline for selecting your multivitamin/mineral supplement:

### DAILY RDA CHART—VITAMINS AND MINERALS FOR AN AVERAGE, HEALTHY WOMAN

| *Vitamins* | *RDA* | *Minerals* | *RDA* |
|---|---|---|---|
| Vitamin A | 1,000–5,000 IU | Calcium | 1,500 mg |
| Beta-carotene | 15,000 IU | Chromium (GTF) | 200 mcg |
| Vitamin B$_1$ | 50 mg | Copper | 3 mg |
| Vitamin B$_2$ | 50 mg | Iodine | 225 mcg |
| Vitamin B$_3$ (niacin) | 100 mg | Iron (only if a deficiency exists) | 18 mg |
| Vitamin B$_5$ (pantothenic acid) | 100 mg | Magnesium | 400–800 mg |
| Vitamin B$_6$ | 50 mg | Manganese | 10 mg |

### DAILY RDA CHART—VITAMINS AND MINERALS FOR AN AVERAGE, HEALTHY WOMAN

| Vitamins | RDA | Minerals | RDA |
|---|---|---|---|
| Vitamin B$_{12}$ | 300 mcg | Molybdenum | 30 mcg |
| Biotin | 300 mcg | Potassium | 99 mg |
| Choline | 100 mg | Selenium | 200 mcg |
| Folic acid | 800 mcg | Zinc | 50 mg |
| Inositol | 100 mg | | |
| PABA | 50 mg | | |
| Vitamin C | 1,000–3,000 mg | | |
| Vitamin D | 400–800 IU | | |
| Vitamin E | 600 IU | | |
| Vitamin K | 100 mcg | | |

## ANTIOXIDANTS

Our immune protection consists of macrophages, white blood cells, antibodies, lymphatic tissue, and the thymus gland. In recent years, science has uncovered health-destroying substances called *free radicals* that attack the body's defenses, weakening them so that they will not properly protect us. Free radicals can damage healthy cells. The good news is that free radicals are controlled by antioxidants, which neutralize free radicals, thereby preventing the weakening and damaging of our cells. There are three basic sources of free-radical activity. First, free radicals are formed as by-products during exercise and illness and by taking certain medications. The second source is air pollution, smoke, radiation, and pesticides. Finally, free radicals form other free radicals. Antioxidants come to the rescue. Their job is to travel the bloodstream, localize in our cells and organs, and neutralize free radicals. After they neutralize or quench these free radicals, they become inactive and are eliminated from the body. This means we continually need to supply our bodies either through diet or supplementation or both.

The four major antioxidants are pro–vitamin A or beta-carotene, vitamin C, vitamin E, and selenium. These four antioxidant nutrients provide a four-point attack. Pro–vitamin A or beta-carotene quenches singlet oxygen molecules. Vitamin C protects tissues and blood components. Vitamin E protects cell membranes, and selenium is a vital part of antioxidant enzymes. All together, these powerful four *mop up* free radicals as they form and before they do their damage to our system.

## GREEN SUPERFOODS

Green superfoods are supercharged with nutrition. Eating any of these green superfoods is almost like receiving a little transfusion to enhance immunity and promote energy and well-being. They are one of the richest sources of essential nutrients. They are nutritionally more compact or concentrated and potent than regular greens like salads and green vegetables. In addition, green superfoods are purposely grown and harvested to maximize and insure high vitamin, mineral, and amino acid concentrations. The chart below will introduce you to green superfoods that are available in most health food stores across the country.

### Green Superfoods for Maximum Nutrition

*Blue and blue-green algae*
The most potent form of beta-carotene available in the world, blue and blue-green algae are called the perfect superfoods because they are brimming with superior quality proteins, fiber, vitamins, minerals, and enzymes.

*Spirulina*
Spirulina is an alga that is extremely high in protein and rich in B vitamins, amino acids, beta-carotene, and essential fatty acids. It is easy to digest, so it boosts energy quickly and sustains it for long periods of time.

*Barley grass*

Barley grass contains vitamins, minerals, proteins, enzymes, and chlorophyll. It contains vitamin C, vitamin $B_{12}$, and more calcium than cow's milk. It also helps inflammatory conditions of the stomach and digestive system.

*Wheat grass*

Wheat grass has been used around the world to alleviate many serious diseases and to rebuild, cleanse, and strengthen the body because of its incredible nutritional value. Fifteen pounds of wheat grass is equivalent to almost four hundred pounds of the most perfectly grown vegetables.

*Kyo-Green*

Kyo-Green, by Wakunaga of America, is my all-time favorite green superfood because of the synergism of the ingredients. Kyo-Green contains barley, wheat grass, chlorella, and kelp. This is a potent formula that helps cleanse the bloodstream, detoxify the system, and supply the body with minerals, enzymes, and many important nutrients providing energy for enhanced daily performance. Together these ingredients do so much more for your body than any of the green superfoods alone. This is what synergism is. I recommend that you have a green drink each day!

## POWER MUSHROOMS

In my quest for wellness, I used what I call power mushrooms. Now, the interest in these same mushrooms has literally...mushroomed! Researchers have found that certain types of mushrooms are filled with a grocery list of substances that may help in fighting disease. Most exciting is that they boost immunity, and some even may be effective against cancer and heart disease. Researchers have discovered that mushrooms produce many beneficial compounds that help their survival against other fungi and microbes. The same substances that mushrooms use for defense can help humans as well. Mushrooms contain compounds known as *polysaccharides*, which spark the immune system by helping the body to create and are immune system warriors that destroy invaders and may halt tumor growth.

It is thought that incorporating any of the power mushrooms into your diet will result in dramatic recoveries because of the synergism with the immune system. According to author Christopher Hobbs in his book *Medicinal Mushrooms*, the chemical steroids and terpenes that mushrooms also contain are thought to help fight the formation of cancerous tumors.[3] By adding one of these power mushrooms to your body-balancing program, you will be adding one more powerful weapon to enhance your immune system.

## POWER MUSHROOMS

- *Reishi*—stimulates immunity, has antitumor and anti-inflammatory properties, and helps to alleviate arthritis.
- *Shiitake*—has possible antiviral, anticancer properties and is an energizer. It is also delicious when used in cooking.
- *Maitake*—has antitumor properties; may protect liver and lower blood pressure. It contains beta-glucans, which are chemicals that boost immunity.[4]

## HERBS

These time-tested and approved plants are truly gifts from God. He has given us every herb of the field for the healing and strengthening of our bodies. Many of our modern-day medicines are derived from herbs! Researchers all over the world know that herbs are very powerful and very effective. Research is ongoing as to how and why herbs can bring balance and healing to our lives. In Europe, herbs have been used for centuries, and they continue to be used on a daily basis. Europeans have confidence in herbal therapy. Now Americans are embracing herbs as a way to prevent or to treat illness. I must stress, however, that education is key when it comes to taking herbs. They are powerful and must be treated with respect. Physicians are now seeing patients who are taking herbal remedies along with their prescribed medications. This can be very dangerous because there can be very real, very dangerous interactions. Some can be life threatening.

Let's begin with a little Herbology 101. There are three basic types of herbs:

- *Food grade:* Food-grade herbs are taken on a daily basis to support the body, cleanse the system, and promote balance. They have a virtually unlimited margin for error (meaning they can be eaten in almost any amount with no reversal of benefits).
- *Medicinal grade:* Medicinal herbs are used in time of crisis, such as cold, flu, or infection. These herbs are used for short periods of time; otherwise, a reversal of benefits may occur.
- *Poisonous:* Poisonous herbs bring very short-term, specific benefits, but they have no margin for error; if misused at all, they will cause a quick and persistent decline in health and possible death.

For more information about the use of natural herbs, see my book *Natural Health Remedies*, chapter two.[5]

## ENZYME SUPPLEMENTATION

*Enzyme supplementation* can make a world of difference in a woman's body. Many of my former clients noticed several improvements. Some were subtle, while some were more dramatic. Most commonly reported was an increase in energy. In addition, sleep improved, and bloating and gas became a thing of the past. As digestion improves, you may lose that "menopot," or excess weight around your middle. The heavy

feeling after a meal will be gone and will be replaced by a lighter, more comfortable feeling. This is simply the result of your digestive system being restocked with ample digestive enzymes. No extra energy will be expended by the body on the digestive process because the enzymes have lightened the workload.

Always remember: the food that you eat is *fuel*. It should energize you, not sideline you with fatigue and bloat. A woman is only as healthy and beautiful physically as what she is able to assimilate and eliminate. Enzyme supplementation will help you to do both. While it is possible to receive enzymes from raw foods that we eat, such as mangoes, papayas, bananas, avocados, and pineapple, I strongly suggest that you make sure that you are "enzymatically insured" by supplementing your body with digestive enzymes from a plant source.

> *Dr. Janet's Recommendation:*
>
> If you don't make enough enzymes— take them!

Plant enzymes support digestion. Enzymes must be in a proper pH in order to be activated. Plant-based enzymes are considered most effective because they have the ability to function under the entire range of gastric pHs that occur throughout the entire digestive system. An ideal plant-based enzyme formula should contain the following:

- Protease (digests protein)
- Amylase (digests starches)
- Lipase (digests fats)
- Lactase (digests milk sugar)
- Cellulase (digests plant fiber)
- Invertase (digests refined sugar)
- Phytase (breaks down phytic acid)

The usual recommendation is to take two plant enzymes at the beginning of every meal.

## TAKE THIS ENZYME TEST

Look at the following chart to determine which enzymes you need to start adding to your program for balance.

*Amylase Deficiency*

- ☐ Breaking out of the skin, rash
- ☐ Hypoglycemia
- ☐ Depression
- ☐ Mood swings
- ☐ Allergies
- ☐ PMS
- ☐ Hot flashes
- ☐ Fatigue
- ☐ Cold hands and feet
- ☐ Neck and shoulder aches
- ☐ Sprue
- ☐ Inflammation

*Protease Deficiency*

- ☐ Back weakness
- ☐ Fungal forms
- ☐ Constipation
- ☐ High blood pressure
- ☐ Insomnia
- ☐ Hearing problems
- ☐ Parasites
- ☐ Gum disorders
- ☐ Gingivitis

*Lipase Deficiency*

- ☐ Aching feet

- ☐ Arthritis
- ☐ Bladder problems
- ☐ Cystitis
- ☐ Acne
- ☐ Gallbladder stress
- ☐ Gallstones
- ☐ Hay fever
- ☐ Prostate problems
- ☐ Psoriasis
- ☐ Urinary weakness
- ☐ Constipation
- ☐ Diarrhea
- ☐ Heart problems

*Combination Deficiency*

- ☐ Chronic allergies
- ☐ Common colds
- ☐ Diverticulitis
- ☐ Irritable bowel
- ☐ Chronic fatigue
- ☐ Sinus infection
- ☐ Immune depressed conditions

## IMMUNE SYSTEM HEALTH

Your immune system is a complex system that depends on the interaction of many different cells, organs, and proteins. Its function is to identify and eliminate foreign substances that invade the body. Vital components of the immune system include the thymus glands, bone marrow, lymphatic system, the liver, and the spleen. When your immune system is experiencing imbalance, there is a host of symptoms that can alert you to the need to take the necessary steps to healing. These include:

- Chronic respiratory problems
- Fatigue
- Allergies
- Yeast overgrowth
- Frequent colds and flu
- Swollen glands
- Asthma
- Skin rashes
- Digestive complaints
- Frequent headaches

In today's society, it is becoming increasingly difficult to keep your immune system strong. Without a strong immune system, you are more susceptible to illness. Your immune system deals with many pathogens on a daily basis (yeasts, parasites, fungi, and viruses), as well as many antigens (pollen, chemicals, drugs, malignant cells, and more). Your immune system is the greatest pharmacy in the world, making more than one hundred billion types of medicines known as *antibodies* to attack just about any unwanted germ or virus that enters your body. Best of all, all of the medicines made by your *internal pharmacy* do not produce side effects, they are free, and they are the most powerful healing agents known to man. Your immune system has only one requirement: the right raw materials to produce the internal medicines to safeguard you from illness. The following recommendations will help you to fortify yourself in times of stress, lighten the load on your immune system, and list for you what nutrient will support and strengthen immunity.

## STRENGTHEN YOUR IMMUNE SYSTEM

*Dietary guidelines to support your immune system*
Eat as close to the *original garden* as possible by choosing:

- Fresh fruits and vegetables
- Garlic and onions (boost immunity)
- High-fiber foods
- Seafood
- Yogurt and kefir
- Avoid sugary foods (pies, cakes), which depress immunity.
- Avoid fried foods, red meat, and refined foods.

*Supplements to support immunity*

The following herbs and natural remedies will help your body to achieve balance in your immune system:

- A cup of green tea
- Moducare (a plant sterol by Natural Balance)
- Bio-K liquid acidophilus
- Vitamin A: a powerful thymus builder
- Vitamin $B_6$ (P5P, pyriodoxal-5-phosphate): many women lack the enzymes to convert vitamin $B_6$ to its active form. P5P is the most bioavailable form of Vitamin $B_6$.
- B complex
- Vitamin C: an antibacterial, antiviral, anticarcinogenic agent and a powerful natural antihistamine
- Vitamin E (d-alpha tocopheryl succinate, natural vitamin E): known as the "fountain of youth." Vitamin E is an active antioxidant with many protective benefits.
- A daily green drink: chlorella, spirulina, kelp, Chlorophyll Liquid, Barley Green, Kyo-Green
- Milk thistle extract
- $CoQ_{10}$: 100 mg daily, a powerful antioxidant that is excellent for health and essential for optimal immune function
- Alpha lipoic acid (thioctic acid): has potent

antioxidant action in almost all tissues of the body
- L-glutathione: the most potent free-radical fighter and detoxifier
- Selenium (selenomethionine): required by the body to make glutathione
- Zinc citrate: enhances the thymus and promotes thymic hormone production
- Plant enzymes with each meal: enhance digestion and assimilation
- Raw thymus glandular
- Ester C: 3,000 mg daily
- Probiotics: for immune strength
- Magnesium: magnesium-deficient cells release more pro-inflammatory cytokines, which then cause more free-radical production and further damage.

*Supporting white blood cell activity*
- Lactoferrin
- Beta-glucan
- Echinacea
- Olive leaf extract
- Astragalus
- Power mushrooms: maitake, shiitake, and/or reishi

*Lifestyle changes to boost your immunity and achieve balance*
- Rest enough.
- Stop smoking.
- Use massage therapy.
- Start to exercise regularly.
- Get fifteen minutes of early morning sunlight daily.
- Laugh with friends.
- Practice deep breathing.
- Deepen your prayer life.

## CHRONIC FATIGUE SYNDROME

Chronic fatigue syndrome is a disorder characterized by feelings of debilitation and lack of energy. This condition has a variety of causes. Researchers have found that a number of viruses are actually involved, including the Epstein-Barr virus, cytomegalovirus, and herpes simplex. Parasites and candida albicans are often found as part of the clinical picture as well. Exhausted adrenal glands and lowered immunity set the stage for this medically incurable viral condition. Most victims are women, usually between the ages of thirty and fifty. Most often sufferers are A-type personalities—overachievers, outgoing, independent, and self-reliant. They often have heightened stress levels and lowered adrenal health. Therefore, the natural remedies for this condition focus on building adrenal health, eliminating yeast and parasites, and boosting immune function.

*Dr. Janet's Recommendation:*

Plant sterols and sterolins have been clinically proven to restore, strengthen, and balance your body's immune system, with a clinically proven ratio of 100:1. They are a very important supplement. I recommend Moducare, available at your local health food store.

There are three stages to this disease. The first stage is recognized by debilitating fatigue. It may begin as merely a craving for more rest and can progress to a need for bed rest for up to six months. The sufferer will have a low-grade fever, sore throat, muscle weakness, gastrointestinal problems, and sore lymph nodes.

The second stage of chronic fatigue syndrome brings more symptoms. Sufferers will develop a ringing in the ears, accompanied by depression, irritability, allergies, vertigo, and sharp muscle aches. The person will be plagued with low blood sugar (hypoglycemia). One of these second-stage symptoms—tinnitus, or ringing in the ears—can be remedied by following the protocol on page 104.

The third stage of chronic fatigue syndrome adds night sweats, frequent infections, weight loss and accompanying loss of appetite, extreme fatigue, fainting, extremely low immunity, heart palpitations, and nervous system disorders.

Fortunately, there are natural health remedies that can help overcome this debilitating, fatigue-producing ailment. These include dietary guidelines, herbal remedies, and important lifestyle changes.

### Overcoming Chronic Fatigue Syndrome

Follow these dietary guidelines:

- Avoid refined sugars, alcohol, dairy, and wheat.
- Eat fresh foods: brown rice, high fiber, yogurt, dark leafy vegetables, prunes, wheat germ, vegetable juices, garlic, and onions.

Incorporate these natural remedies:

- Digestive plant enzymes
- B complex
- Magnesium chloride: 800 mg
- Royal jelly
- Reishi mushroom capsules
- Carnitine: 2,000 mg daily
- Adrenal glandular
- Ester C: 3,000–5,000 mg
- A green drink daily
- Olive leaf extract
- Grapefruit seed extract
- Candex, for yeast eradication
- Milk thistle extract
- Bio-K acidophilus
- Astragalus
- $CoQ_{10}$: 100 mg daily

Make these healthy lifestyle changes:

- Have a massage at least three times monthly.
- Manage stress.

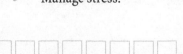

- Begin a walking program.
- Spend fifteen minutes in morning sunlight.

---

🍃 *Dr. Janet's Protocol to Relieve the Ringing in Your Ears*

## To Help Relieve Ringing:

- Gingko biloba for three months
- Bilberry capsules
- Ginger capsules
- $CoQ_{10}$, 200 mg two times daily
- Take a fiber supplement daily.
- Use Sytrino to help lower cholesterol.
- Chromium picolinate will help lower triglycerides.
- Try HearAll by Dr. Bob Martin (an all-natural formula).

## Nutrients to Combat Stress Associated With Tinnitus:

- B complex
- L-theanine, up to three times daily
- Calcium: 1,500 mg
- Magnesium: 800 mg
- $B_{12}$ sublingual: 2,500 mcg daily
- Black cohosh to repair nerves
- Royal jelly daily

For more information about finding balance in your immune system, read my book *90-Day Immune System Makeover*. In addition to fortifying your immune system with specific supplements, you must address any unhealthy lifestyle habits now. You need to address life situations that are draining you of health and energy, such as being around a certain person or group, in a particular building or environment at work or at home, or in some other specific situation that leaves you feeling excessively tired or stressed. Finding out what drains you and tires you will help you to determine what external factors may be contributing to low immunity. It will also restore balance to your life emotionally.

Getting regular exercise, getting adequate rest, and having a healthy mental and spiritual life will further help to insure your immunity. These three guidelines will ensure that you are a woman balanced by nature—physically, emotionally, and spiritually.

Weight control is so important to a woman's health and happiness that I have dedicated an entire chapter to this topic. A woman's weight issues cannot be healed completely until she has accepted her body unconditionally. A large component of body balance is to regain the body acceptance and self-esteem that a woman lost as she entered adolescence. Before I give you my guidelines for achieving your optimal weight, I want to give you five steps to refer to often for three weeks as you implement my weight loss recommendations.

### STEPS TO DEVELOPING BETTER WEIGHT CONTROL

1. Try to befriend your body just as it is, and list five things you like about your body right now. Remind yourself of those items the next time you are feeling self-critical.
2. Perfect your posture; stand tall, and walk with grace. Dress to play up your best features.
3. Continue to take charge of your health. Get in the habit of scanning your body once a day, paying attention to areas in which you feel pain or tension. Long before an illness develops, your body often sends you warning signals. Paying attention to them will help you to maintain a high energy level as well as prevent a bigger health crisis. Keep

up with medical screening tests—blood pressure, breast, skin, and cholesterol checks; Pap smears; and dental checkups.

4. Do not deprive yourself. Make sure you eat plenty of fruits, vegetables, and whole grains for lifetime protection from all sorts of chronic diseases, as well as to help keep your weight in balance. When you crave chocolate, indulge! Just don't overdo it!

5. Everyone gets overstressed from time to time, whether from family obligations, work, or just too much to do. When your body and soul become depleted, you need rest, along with emotional and spiritual sustenance to get back on an even keel. Make time to catch up on your sleep. Spend quality time with a good friend. Enjoy a romantic dinner. Escape for a long weekend alone, or spend a day gardening. Whatever works for you is fine; just make it a habit. You are worth it![1]

Weight loss has become a national obsession in America. Many women are constantly trying to lose weight through diets, exercise, herbal remedies, behavior modification, and more. It is unfortunate that this obsession is often triggered by concerns about appearance instead of health. Sadly, women often turn to fashion rather than health when it comes to determining their ideal weight.

As mentioned throughout this book, the only way to enjoy optimal health and body balance is with a lifestyle overhaul. Attaining your perfect weight requires you to do the same. You must approach this overhaul one step at a time. Sure, weight loss will happen if you limit your food intake to 1,500 calories a day, but the weight loss will be short term and hard to maintain. The truth is, the right foods and nutritional supplements when combined with an exercise program can bring your body chemistry into balance, making it easier for you to lose weight, maintain the weight loss, and become healthier than ever before!

There are three important numbers that will help to determine whether or not your current weight and body shape are contributing to your chance of developing heart disease, diabetes, cancer, arthritis, incontinence, polycystic breasts, cancer, gallstones, stroke, and hypertension.

First of all, let's determine your *body mass index*, commonly known as your BMI. Your BMI is a more accurate method than a scale for determining how much of the body is fat and how much is muscle and bone. To determine your BMI, simply multiply your body weight by 703. Divide that amount by your height in inches, and then divide your answer one more time by your height in inches. A healthy BMI is between 18.5 and 24.9. Numbers from 25 to 29.9 indicate overweight. Any number 30 or above indicates obesity.

> *Dr. Janet's Recommendation:*
>
> Chocolate craving? Take 250 mg of magnesium.[2]

You should also measure your *waist/hip ratio*. Simply measure around the fullest part of your buttocks. Then measure your waist at the narrowest part of your torso. Now divide your waist measurement by your hip measurement. A healthy ratio is less than 0.8. The ideal ratio is 0.74. If your ratio is greater than 0.85, you are at risk for all of the health risks I mentioned above.

To find out your *percentage of body fat*, you may purchase a scale that measures your weight and body fat percentage (they are fairly accurate), or you can have it measured at your health club or by your physician. A body fat percentage between 20 and 28 is considered healthy for women in their perimenopausal or menopausal years, while 12 to 23 percent is ideal for younger women.

If your numbers are in the healthy range, good for you. If not, the good news is that you can bring your numbers into the healthy range by making the following lifestyle changes or addressing the following areas.

## GAINING WEIGHT? CHECK YOUR THYROID

It is estimated that one in four American women can attribute their weight gain to low or borderline low thyroid hormones. Women with healthy thyroid function burn calories more efficiently. The following symptoms accompany low thyroid hormone production, also known as hypothyroidism: fatigue, depression, weakness, weight gain, high cholesterol levels, low body temperature, and hair loss. When your thyroid hormone levels are restored, your energy level, weight, temperature, muscle strength, cholesterol, emotional health, and more will improve. If you can relate to any of these symptoms, see your health-care provider and ask for a thyroid health screening blood test, TSH (thyroid stimulating hormone), Free T4, and T3 tests.

There are natural supplements that can help correct thyroid dysfunction. L-tyrosine plays a crucial role in supporting the thyroid gland. Tyrosine boosts your metabolism as well as acting as the precursor for dopamine, norepinephrine, and epinephrine, which are nervous system chemicals that affect metabolism, mental alertness, and energy levels. Tyrosine can be taken in supplement form with a meal that contains protein. If your doctor finds that you are suffering from hypothyroidism, you may take L-tyrosine with your thyroid medication. Make sure to keep your thyroid monitored with periodic blood tests. You may be able to reduce or eliminate the need for the medication.

To test yourself for an underactive thyroid, take this self-test developed by Broda Barnes, MD, author of *Hypothroidism: The Unsuspected Illness.* Keep a basal thermometer by your bedside. Before turning in, shake down the thermometer and place it within easy reach of your bed. In the morning, before arising, lie still, and place the thermometer under your armpit for ten minutes. Keep quiet and still—any motion can upset the reading. Record your readings for the next ten days:

|  | *Date* | *Temperature* |
|---|---|---|
| 1. | _____ | _____ |
| 2. | _____ | _____ |

3. _____          _____
4. _____          _____
5. _____          _____
6. _____          _____
7. _____          _____
8. _____          _____
9. _____          _____
10. _____          _____

Women should not take a reading during the first few days of their menstrual cycle or on the middle day of their cycle because body temperature fluctuates during those times. A normal reading is between 97.8 and 98.2 degrees Fahrenheit. A temperature below 97.6 degrees Fahrenheit may indicate low thyroid function.

## INFLAMMATION

Trauma and bacterial, viral, and allergic reactions can manifest as swelling, fluid retention, and bloating, all equaling weight gain. To find out if inflammation is contributing to your current weight or a recent weight gain, follow these recommendations. You will know quickly as you see the number on your scale go down.

- Eliminate dairy products, and choose rice, soy, or almond milk. Choose rice, soy, or almond cheese.
- Eliminate wheat; use millet, rice, oat, amaranth, or quinoa breads or crackers, and pastas made from rice, quinoa, or buckwheat. Try millet, oat, or rice cookies!

Adding the following natural anti-inflammatories will help bring down inflammation as you eliminate wheat and dairy.

- Quercetin: a natural antihistamine, 500 mg twice daily
- Bromelain: digestive enzyme known for anti-inflammatory properties, 1000 mg following a meal

- MSM: most powerful anti-inflammatory from natural medicine, 250 mg of MSM granules, three times daily with meals
- Chromium: will help to increase lean body mass and decrease your percentage of body fat
- Fiber: enhances weight loss and helps to curb cravings and feelings of hunger. In addition, it helps to eliminate wastes that are released during weight loss. Take 4–6 Tbsp. of ground flaxseed daily.
- Add these fat burners: L-carnitine, 1000 mg daily; magnesium, 400–800 mg daily; green tea, 100 mg of green tea catechins three times daily.
- CLA (conjugated linoleic acid): 3000 mg daily, but do not take late in the afternoon or evening.

## MANAGE STRESS

Anxiety can cause you to overeat. To determine the level of anxiety you are experiencing in your life, take the following anxiety self-test. It will assess your symptoms and help you to know whether anxiety is one of the health robbers with which you may be dealing.

### HAMILTON ANXIETY SCALE (HAMA)

Mark only the applicable box in each case.[3]

**Anxious**—worry, expectation of the worst, fearful expectations, irritability

☐ Not present

☐ Mild

☐ Moderate

☐ Strong

☐ Very strong

**Tension**—feeling of tension, exhaustibility, nervousness, tendency toward crying, trembling, feeling of uneasiness, restlessness, and incapacity to relax

- ☐ Not present
- ☐ Mild
- ☐ Moderate
- ☐ Strong
- ☐ Very strong

**Fear**—fear of darkness, strangers, of being left alone, of animals, of traffic, of crowds

- ☐ Not present
- ☐ Mild
- ☐ Moderate
- ☐ Strong
- ☐ Very strong

**Insomnia**—difficulty in falling asleep, difficulty in sleeping through the night, not being well rested, exhaustion upon awakening, dreams, nightmares

- ☐ Not present
- ☐ Mild
- ☐ Moderate
- ☐ Strong
- ☐ Very strong

**Impairment of intellectual performance**—difficulty in concentration, memory loss

- ☐ Not present
- ☐ Mild
- ☐ Moderate
- ☐ Strong
- ☐ Very strong

**Depressive mood**—loss of interest, decreased enjoyment of hobbies, despondency, early waking, daily mood fluctuations

- ☐ Not present
- ☐ Mild
- ☐ Moderate
- ☐ Strong
- ☐ Very strong

**General somatic symptoms (muscular)**—muscle pain, muscle spasm, muscle stiffness, myoclonic spasm, teeth grinding, shaky voice, increased muscle tonus

- ☐ Not present
- ☐ Mild
- ☐ Moderate
- ☐ Strong
- ☐ Very strong

**General somatic symptoms (sensorial)**—tinnitus (ringing in the ears), blurred vision, hot flashes and cold shivers, feeling of weakness, "pins and needles"

- ☐ Not present
- ☐ Mild
- ☐ Moderate
- ☐ Strong
- ☐ Very strong

**Cardiovascular problems**—tachycardia, heart palpitation, breast pain, venous throbbing, fainting feeling, irregular heartbeat

- ☐ Not present
- ☐ Mild
- ☐ Moderate
- ☐ Strong
- ☐ Very strong

**Respiratory symptoms**—feeling of pressure of tightness in the chest, feelings of asphyxiation, loss of breath, dyspnea

☐ Not present

☐ Mild

☐ Moderate

☐ Strong

☐ Very strong

**Gastrointestinal symptoms**—difficulty in swallowing, flatulence, stomach pain, pain before or after eating, heartburn, sensation of repletion, belching, nausea, vomiting, intestinal rumbling, diarrhea, loss of weight, constipation

☐ Not present

☐ Mild

☐ Moderate

☐ Strong

☐ Very strong

**Urogenital symptoms**—frequent urination, urge to pass water, amenorrhea, menorrhagia, development of frigidity, loss of libido, impotence

☐ Not present

☐ Mild

☐ Moderate

☐ Strong

☐ Very strong

**Neuro-vegetative symptoms**—dryness of the mouth, blushing, paleness, tendency to perspire, vertigo, tension headache, "goose-flesh"

☐ Not present

☐ Mild

☐ Moderate

☐ Strong

☐ Very strong

**Behavior during interview (if clinical visit)**—fidgetiness, restlessness, pacing, hand tremor, eyebrow furrowing, weary face, difficulty in or rapid breathing, pale face, air swallowing, eyelid twitching, nervous tics, perspiration

☐ Not present

☐ Mild

☐ Moderate

☐ Strong

☐ Very strong

Score each answer as follows:

- Not present: 0
- Mild: 1
- Moderate: 2
- Strong: 3
- Very strong: 4

*Total Score* _____

A score of 18–24 may indicate mild anxiety; 25–29, moderate anxiety; a score of over 30 may indicate severe anxiety.

I have found this test to be invaluable as a tool not only to educate anxiety-ridden individuals on the very real anxiety epidemic, but also as a guide where progress can be charted.

If you are dealing with stress and anxiety, replace all foods that will magnify your symptoms, such as caffeine, chocolate, coffee, black tea, sugar, and alcohol, with calming foods such as brown rice, poultry, fish, vegetables, and whole grains.

Now you are ready to begin taking your important first healthy steps toward better weight control.

## DR. JANET'S WEIGHT LOSS PROGRAM

*Guidelines*

1. Eat three meals and two snacks daily. This will keep blood sugar levels stable.
2. Watch your portion size. Make a fist, which is the amount of protein you should eat at each meal. Two fists is the amount of fruit, vegetables, and healthy grains eaten at each meal. One thumb is the amount of healthy fat at each meal (olive oil or flaxseed oil).
3. Eat protein at each meal.
4. Include fish in your diet regularly.
5. Eat only lean meat, and eat it sparingly.
6. Include eggs and egg whites in your diet.
7. Learn to enjoy the health benefits of soy and tofu.
8. Drink delicious whey protein shakes.
9. Consume refined grains with caution! Many women are *carb sensitive*, and this triggers binge eating.
10. Eat plenty of fruits and vegetables at each meal: five servings daily, ½ cup equals one serving.
11. Drink plenty of water daily. It helps your body get rid of toxins.

### BODY WEIGHT/WATER CALCULATOR

Total body weight           _____

Divide by 2           _____

Daily ounces of water per day           _____

MAKE HEALTHY CHOICES

| Protein | Carbohydrates: Fruits | Carbohydrates: Vegetables/Grains | Fats |
|---|---|---|---|
| Eggs | Apples | Broccoli | Olive oil |
| Egg whites | Oranges | Green beans | Vegetable oil |
| Fish, tuna, salmon | Grapefruit | Cauliflower | Almonds |
| Chicken (skinless) | Strawberries | Spinach | Walnuts |
| Turkey (skinless) | Pears | Asparagus | Avocados |
| Lean meat | Peaches | Zucchini | |
| Whey protein powder | Plums | Grain | |
| Tofu | | Barley | |
| | | Oatmeal | |
| | | Rye | |
| | | Brown rice | |

The key thing to remember about weight loss is balance. Make sure each meal and snack contain carbohydrates to provide glucose for your brain, protein to provide amino acids needed to build and repair body protein and release glucagon (your fat-burning hormone), and fat to supply fatty acids needed for blood sugar control, appetite suppression, and hormone production.

## HOW TO DESIGN YOUR MEAL

I am suggesting a three-week weight control program for you to use to bring balance to this area of your life. You will want to select one high-quality protein, two carbohydrates (one fruit and one vegetable), and one serving of good fat at each meal. Be sure that you chart your progress at each meal. You can make photocopies of the daily eating plan on page 120, and journal each day of your three-week journey to balance.

I recommend the following dietary guidelines to help you choose the foods that can most help you achieve balance in your weight. A high-fiber diet is necessary. Fiber improves the excretion of fat, improves glucose tolerance, and gives you a feeling of fullness and satisfaction.

Emphasize the following foods: brown rice, tuna, chicken, white fish, fresh fruits and vegetables, high-protein lean foods, lentils, beans, whole-grain bread, and turkey. Add healthy fats to your diet, such as olive oil, safflower oil, and flax oil. Whey protein shakes help to keep blood sugar stabilized. These actually improve fat burning. Avoid sugars and snack foods that contain salt and fat, such as potato chips, ice cream, candy, cookies, cake, breakfast cereals that are high in sugar, and soda. Do not choose high-fat cheeses, sour cream, whole milk, butter, mayonnaise, fried foods, peanut butter (unless it is natural), or rich salad dressings. Do not drink alcoholic beverages at all—they are high in calories.

Eat several small meals daily instead of skipping meals and eating one big meal daily. You want to give your body even burning fuel throughout the day. Otherwise, your body will store fat instead of burn it for "survival."

As you journal each day of this three-week program, keep a summary of your weight loss. Journal the things that you did that you believe helped you to lose weight, and journal the things that may have hindered you from taking off the weight.

Keep a record of the vitamins and supplements you included in your weight-loss plan. I recommend the following to you:

## SUPPLEMENTS
Fat Burners:

- Green tea or green tea capsules as a thermogenic
  White willow bark, also a thermogenic
- CLA
- Chromium picolinate, 200–400 mcg daily, to restore blood sugar balance
- Pyruvate: 6–8 gm per day with diluted fruit juice
- Chickweed: acts as an appetite suppressant
- L-tyrosine or kelp: for thyroid support and to raise serotonin levels
- L-carnitine: promotes lean muscle
- Drink plenty of water (one-half your body weight in ounces)

## THREE WEEKS TO HEALTHY WEIGHT LOSS

*Starting weight:* _____ *Day* _____ *Date* _____

Breakfast

      Protein _____

      Carbohydrate _____

      Fat _____

      Water _____

Small snack

      Protein _____

      Carbohydrate _____

      Fat _____

      Water _____

Lunch

      Protein _____

      Carbohydrate _____

      Fat _____

      Water _____

Small snack

      Protein _____

      Carbohydrate _____

      Fat _____

      Water _____

Dinner

      Protein _____

      Carbohydrate _____

      Fat _____

      Water _____

Exercise: Describe your workout (exercise daily)

_____

_____

      Total minutes _____ Water: _____ total ounces

Emotions (monitor your mood)

_____

_____

*Important: Leave three hours between your last meal and bedtime.*

Anti-inflammatory supplements:
 Bromelain
 Quercetin
 MSM

CLA is another supplement that helps with fat loss. It decreases fat deposition, especially in the abdomen. Red meat, butter, and cheese used to contain abundant amounts of CLA. Today there is less CLA in dairy products because most cows are artificially fattened in feedlots rather than by grazing on grass. Americans consume less red meat, butter, and dairy foods today, and only a portion of CLA is obtained through these food sources compared to previous generations.

CLA has shown strong anticancer properties, being particularly effective in inhibiting breast and prostate tumors, as well as colorectal, stomach, and skin cancer, including melanoma. Even low concentrations of CLA can inhibit cancer cell growth.[4]

CLA has also been shown to improve the lean mass to body fat ratio, enhancing muscle growth.[5] The amount of CLA used in human weight-loss studies was 3,000 mg of pure CLA. I recommend you take at least 3,000–4,000 mg daily, but be sure to take it all at once, early in the day.

### LIFESTYLE CHANGES TO SUPPORT WEIGHT LOSS
It will be important for you to make the following lifestyle changes to be successful in your weight-loss program:

- Avoid fad diets, which do not work and give only temporary results.
- Eat slowly and chew your food properly. Take time to taste your food.
- Do not eat when you are upset, lonely, or depressed.
- Chewing gum can stimulate your appetite, so you should leave it alone while trying to lose weight.
- Drink plenty of water.

- Stay regular. Do not become constipated.
- Begin a walking program (after dinner is best). See chapter five for suggestions for your walking program.

If you are trying to change your daily habits without a little help from your friends, you might be missing something very important. A study in the *Journal of Consulting and Clinical Psychology* found that 95 percent of those who signed up for a weight-loss program with three friends completed the four-month program, compared with 76 percent of those who registered alone. Those who signed up with their friends not only lost more weight than their counterparts, but they also kept it off longer.[6]

## THE CORTISOL-OBESITY CONNECTION

Emerging studies suggest a link between central obesity, marked by abdominal fat, and a high waist-to-hip ratio to elevated cortisol levels. Exercise, stress-management techniques such as relaxation and medication, and nutritional supplements can help you manage stress and lower cortisol to promote optimal health and longevity. The following are scientifically supported techniques that can help support a healthy response to stress.

*Behavioral techniques to lower stress and manage high cortisol levels:*

- Exercise 30–45 minutes of both anaerobic (resistance training) and aerobic (jogging, cycling) every other day.
- Meditation relaxation: 15–30 minutes daily

*Supplements to reduce high cortisol levels secondary to stress:*

- Vitamin C: 1,000–3,000 mg a day
- Fish oil (omega-3 fatty acids): 1–4 gm a day
- Phosphatidylserine: 300–800 mg a day
- Rhodiola rosea: 100–200 mg a day, standardized extract
- Ginseng: 100–300 mg a day, standardized extract
- Ginkgo biloba: 100–200 mg a day, standardized extract

- DHEA: 25–50 mg a day (any hormone supplementation should be monitored by your physician)[7]

Gradual weight loss is more permanent than quick weight loss. Be patient. The results are more likely to be permanent if the weight loss is a daily gradual process of lifestyle and dietary changes.

## WEIGHT-LOSS SUCCESS TIPS

As you get started with your weight-loss program, follow these simple tips:

- Do not deprive yourself. Eat healthy.
- An occasional slice of pie will not ruin your progress. Just remember—occasionally is the key.
- Ask for support. Make your friends and family aware of your weight-loss goal, and enlist their support.
- Turn to friends, family, and prayer to help work through any personal problems so that you will not turn to food for comfort.
- Monitor your health. Keep up with health screenings, blood pressure, cholesterol screenings, Pap smears, mammograms, dental checkups, skin exams, and chiropractic evaluation.
- Find purpose: Fill your life with things that mean more to you than food. Volunteer at church, participate in an outreach program, call family members or your best friend, and get involved with passion. Find a cause to believe in, and dive in!
- Pray. A rich prayer life helps to decrease stress, social pressures, and depression, all of which contribute to overeating.

# CHAPTER 5

# THE IMPORTANCE OF EXERCISE

Exercise is a valuable tool for bringing balance to a woman's life. When a woman engages in moderate exercise on a regular basis, at least three times a week for thirty minutes, she will reduce stress, promote endocrine health, improve circulation, elevate her mood, and provide oxygenation to tight, constricted muscles. But while this chapter will address the advantages of physical exercise, let me remind you that in order for true balance and well-being to occur, your emotional and spiritual health must be given as much attention as you devote to your physical frame. While working on this book, I read this statement, one I was prompted to pass on to you: "There is little point in maintaining the temple if the sanctuary inside is in ruins."[1]

Exercise does energize you and lift your spirit. It also aids in detoxification. In addition, there are obvious medical and psychological benefits, such as boosting immunity and preventing obesity and all of its attendant health risks, including heart disease, high blood pressure, high cholesterol, and more.

High blood pressure, or hypertension, is often called the "silent killer," because a person can be suffering from high blood pressure and not have any noticeable symptoms. The exact cause is sometimes hard to pinpoint. Since high blood pressure is so prevalent among people who do not exercise regularly, I want to give you some recommendations that you can use as balancing tools to bring your blood pressure into balance

as you begin your regular exercise program. As you make these dietary and herbal remedies changes, be sure you exercise regularly to keep your stress to a minimum and to lose weight. The walking program we will discuss in this chapter is excellent for helping you reduce high blood pressure.

## Balancing Your Blood Pressure

Hypertension (high blood pressure) is ranked in stages:

|  | *Systolic* | *Diastolic* |
|---|---|---|
| Normal | 120 | 80 |
| Stage I | 140 to 159 | 90 to 99 |
| Stage II | 160 to 179 | 100 to 109 |
| Stage III | 180 to 209 | 110 to 119 |
| Stage IV | 210 or higher | 120 or higher |

Even Stage I hypertension can cause serious health problems, increasing your chances of stroke, heart attack, kidney failure, and more. Take immediate steps to lower your blood pressure if your reading is higher than 120/80.

Follow these dietary guidelines:

- Eat a high-fiber diet.
- Reduce salt consumption, including salty foods like cured, smoked foods, soy sauce, potato chips, and dry soup mixes. Salt promotes fluid retention, which increases blood pressure.
- Avoid caffeine; it raises blood pressure.
- Add garlic, celery, olive oil, and flaxseed oil to your diet.
- Avoid soy sauce, MSG, and canned vegetables.
- Avoid smoked and aged cheeses and meats, chocolate, canned broths, and animal fats.
- Limit sugar intake. It can increase sodium retention.

> Avoid phenylalanine (found in diet foods and drinks) and antihistamines.

There are many natural herbal remedies that can help you lower your blood pressure:

> Arjuna bark: 500 mg three times daily

> Magnesium: 400–800 mg

> Hawthorn: 100–250 mg three times daily

> Vitamin E: 100 IU daily; may be increased to 400–800 IU daily

> B-complex vitamin

> Calcium (citrate): 1,000 mg daily

> Omega-3 fish or flax oils

> Hawthorn extract (especially good for palpitations)

> Gingko biloba (good for boosting circulation)

> Hibiscus tea (clinically proven to lower high blood pressure[2])

> Ester C: 1,000 mg daily in divided doses

> Hyland's Calms Forte tabs (homeopathic remedy to reduce stress)

> Chromium picolinate: 200 mcg if under 150 pounds, and 400 mcg if over 150 pounds, daily

> Potassium as directed

> Fiber supplement

> Milk thistle for liver function

> Garlic, which inhibits platelet aggregation

> Valerian root for stress

> Black cohosh, which calms the cardiovascular system

> Cayenne, a blood pressure normalizer

You may want to invest in a home blood pressure monitor kit in order to monitor your blood pressure. Ideally, your blood pressure should be below 120/80. Hypertension is indicated if your reading rises

to over 140/90. The good news is that you can, in most cases, lower your blood pressure by losing weight and making lifestyle changes

Make a commitment now to stick with an exercise program. But I want you to know that this is a guilt-free zone. The truth is, an exercise program can consume an enormous amount of your time and energy. Exercise enthusiasts contend that exercise provides a wonderful and dependable way to release tension and stress. However, many women go to the expense and effort to join a health club or purchase a piece of home gym equipment and fail to use it. Their intentions are good, but life happens, and many women are faced with other tasks that take precedence over their exercise program. This creates what I call "exercise guilt." Guilt is stressful. While I am going to outline the benefit of exercise in this chapter, I want to offer you this bit of advice. You do NOT have to spend enormous amounts of time, money, and energy on an exercise program that may be stressing you out and defeating its very purpose!

> *Dr. Janet's Recommendation:*
>
> Consider walking, swimming, and slow cycling, which will invite your body, mind, and spirit to play together rather than to work apart.

Women who have lives and bodies that are out of balance do not need another stressor, namely a stressful exercise program! They barely have enough energy to go to work each day, care for the home, and, in extreme cases, are unable to get out of bed! I know from past experience! If you can relate to anything I have just mentioned, then consider making time in your busy schedule to enjoy an evening walk or swim, or get yourself a bicycle and do some slow cycling—all are forms of exercise that will exercise you physically, emotionally, and spiritually.

Now that I have taken the pressure off of you, I will give you reasons why exercise will help to improve your life. The key is moderation and realizing that no one is expecting you to be a triathlete here. These are just plain facts for you to take into consideration as you make exercise a regular part of your health-balancing program.

## WHAT WOULD IT TAKE TO GET YOU MOTIVATED?

Do you enjoy moving your body?

_____

Recall a moment in your life in which you were captivated by the sheer joy of dancing, running, swimming, or jumping. When was the last time you felt this way?

_____

_____

When was the last time that you felt that pleasurable sense of complete relaxation that comes from spending a day immersed in the pleasures of some activity—skiing, hiking, sailing, dancing, or skating?

_____

_____

What types of activities did you enjoy as a child?

_____

_____

As a teenager?

_____

_____

If you do not exercise now, why not?

_____

_____

If you don't exercise now, when did you stop? Why?

_____

_____

Do you feel that you don't have time to exercise? Why not?[3]

_____

_____

There are three main areas of exercise that women need to address. We will take a closer look at each of these areas.

## AEROBIC ACTIVITY

Aerobic exercise is any type of movement such as walking or bicycling that gets your heart pumping and increases your oxygen intake. The good news is that when it comes to achieving a higher level of aerobic fitness, it can be FUN! There are many activities that qualify as aerobic exercise when done for thirty minutes at a time. These include housework and gardening as well as dancing, jumping rope, elliptical training, rowing, swimming, aquatic exercise, aerobic dance class, stair climbing, bicycling, running, and cross-country skiing.

Aerobic exercise can help ward off illness and viral illness, reduce your risk of stroke or coronary artery disease, strengthen your heart muscle, improve blood flow, lower your blood pressure, and lessen the risk of type 2 diabetes. Are you motivated yet?

To receive the full benefit of your aerobic exercise program, you must keep your heart rate in your *target zone*. In order to find your target zone, I have provided a heart rate range chart for you to make your work aerobic workout safe and more effective.

### WORKING HEART RATE RANGE CHART
#### BEATS PER MINUTE (BPM)[3]

| Resting Heart Rate | Age | | | | | | | |
|---|---|---|---|---|---|---|---|---|
| | 30 and Under | 31–40 | 41–45 | 46–50 | 51–55 | 56–60 | 61–65 | Over 65 |
| 50–51 | 140–190 | 130–190 | 130–180 | 120–170 | 120–170 | 120–160 | 110–150 | 110–150 |
| 52–53 | 140–190 | 130–190 | 130–180 | 120–170 | 120–170 | 120–160 | 110–150 | 110–150 |
| 54–56 | 140–190 | 130–190 | 130–180 | 120–170 | 120–170 | 120–160 | 110–150 | 110–150 |
| 57–58 | 140–190 | 130–190 | 130–180 | 130–170 | 120–170 | 120–160 | 110–150 | 110–150 |
| 59–61 | 140–190 | 140–190 | 130–180 | 130–170 | 120–170 | 120–160 | 110–150 | 110–150 |
| 62–63 | 140–190 | 140–190 | 130–180 | 130–170 | 120–170 | 120–160 | 120–150 | 110–150 |
| 64–66 | 140–190 | 140–190 | 130–180 | 130–170 | 130–170 | 120–160 | 120–150 | 110–150 |
| 67–68 | 140–190 | 140–190 | 140–180 | 130–170 | 130–170 | 120–160 | 120–150 | 110–150 |

## WORKING HEART RATE RANGE CHART
### BEATS PER MINUTE (BPM)[3]

| Resting Heart Rate | Age | | | | | | | |
|---|---|---|---|---|---|---|---|---|
| | 30 and Under | 31–40 | 41–45 | 46–50 | 51–55 | 56–60 | 61–65 | Over 65 |
| 69–71 | 150–190 | 140–190 | 140–180 | 130–170 | 130–170 | 120–160 | 120–150 | 120–150 |
| 72–73 | 150–190 | 140–190 | 140–180 | 130–170 | 130–170 | 130–160 | 120–150 | 120–150 |
| 74–76 | 150–190 | 140–190 | 140–180 | 130–170 | 130–170 | 130–160 | 120–150 | 120–150 |
| 77–78 | 150–190 | 140–190 | 140–180 | 130–170 | 130–170 | 130–160 | 120–150 | 120–150 |
| 79–81 | 150–190 | 140–190 | 140–180 | 130–170 | 130–170 | 130–160 | 120–150 | 120–150 |
| 82–83 | 150–190 | 140–190 | 140–180 | 140–170 | 130–170 | 130–160 | 120–150 | 120–150 |
| 84–86 | 150–190 | 150–190 | 140–180 | 140–170 | 130–170 | 130–160 | 120–150 | 120–150 |
| 87–88 | 150–190 | 150–190 | 140–180 | 140–170 | 130–170 | 130–160 | 130–150 | 120–150 |
| 89–91 | 150–190 | 150–190 | 140–180 | 140–170 | 140–170 | 130–160 | 130–150 | 120–150 |

Your target heart rate is 60 percent to 85 percent of your maximum heart rate. Your maximum heart rate is the upper limit of what your cardiovascular system can handle during physical activity. Exercising in your *target zone* will help boost your fitness level and will thereby improve your overall health.

To check your heart rate during aerobic exercise:

1. Stop momentarily.
2. Take your pulse for ten seconds.
3. Multiply this number by six to calculate your beats per minute.[4]

Out of all of the possible aerobic exercise options, I personally enjoy walking. I enjoy a daily walk with a *walking buddy* or alone with a headset and my favorite music. I choose upbeat, fast-paced music when I want to speed-walk, or slower, more contemplative music when I want to walk for long distances.

When engaging in a walking program, you must make sure to wear a good pair of walking shoes that fit properly so that you won't suffer the agony of multiple blisters. In addition, you *must* warm up your muscles

before you embark. You can do this by walking slowly in place or by walking very slowly for about five minutes. After you feel that you have warmed up adequately, make sure to stretch your calf muscles, hamstrings, lower back, and chest in order to prevent any muscle strains or torn ligaments. It can happen!

If you do suffer from muscle pains and aches, try these natural remedies.

### Dr. Janet's Protocol for Muscle Pains and Aches

**Natural Support for Muscle Pains and Aches— Including Arthritis**

- MSM capsules, 800 mg daily
- Calcium/magnesium citrate
- Vitamin D, 1,000 IU
- Magnesium, 400 mg two times daily
- $CoQ_{10}$, 60 mg three times daily
- Have regular massages and take sea salt or Epsom salt baths (2 cups to a tub of water)
- Have a green drink daily

*To reduce inflammation*
- Quercetin, 1,000 mg
- Bromelain, 1,500 mg.
- Dr. Janet's Glucosamine Cream
- Reduce cramping with Hyland's Mag Phos

For extra motivation, why not consider purchasing a pedometer? It simply attaches to your waistband and will record your steps walked by detecting body motion. Your total steps walked are displayed on a screen. Why not keep a personal walking journal of total steps walked?

Remember, optimal results happen in your target zone. You can check your heart rate manually by locating your pulse on your wrist (radial) or on your neck (carotid). Another option would be to purchase an electronic device that records and displays your pulse rate.

## STRENGTH TRAINING

Strength training is very important, especially at midlife, because it is proven to help build bone over time. It can also improve your posture and balance. You can combine strength training with your aerobic activity by using handheld weights or ankle weights when you walk. If you have bone or joint problems, you may do leg lifts, wall push-ups, and traditional push-ups.

Studies have shown that lifting weights two or three times per week increases strength by building muscle mass and bone density. For example, a twelve-month study conducted at Tufts University demonstrated 1 percent gains in hip and spine density, 75 percent increases in strength, and 13 percent increases in dynamic balance with just two days per week of progressive strength training. The control group had losses in both strength and balance.[5] The good news, especially for women, is that strength training can help to prevent long-term medical problems such as osteoporosis.

> *Dr. Janet's Recommendation:*
>
> Rotate workouts to prevent boredom, over-training, and injury.

Strength training uses resistance methods like free weights, weight machines, and resistance bands to build muscles and strength.

### TEN QUICK TIPS TO HELP YOU GET STARTED

1. Remember to warm up. Warming up gives the body a chance to deliver plenty of nutrient-rich blood to areas about to be exercised to actually warm the muscles and lubricate the joints.
2. Stretching increases or maintains muscle flexibility.
3. During the first week of starting an exercise program keep it light. Work on technique and good body mechanics, and slowly work up to heavier weights.
4. Quick tips to maintain good body mechanics: go through the complete range of motion, move slowly and with

control, breathe, and maintain a neutral spine. Never sacrifice form just to add more weight or repetitions.

5.   The intensity of your workout depends on a number of factors, including the number of sets and repetitions, the overall weight lifted, and the rest between sets. You can vary the intensity of your workout to fit your activity level and goals.

6.   Listen to your body. Heart rate is not a good way to determine your intensity when lifting weights; it is important to listen to your body based on an overall sense or feeling of exertion.

7.   The *minimum* amount of strength training recommended by the American College of Sports Medicine is eight to twelve repetitions of eight to ten exercises, at a moderate intensity, two days a week. You will get more overall gains with more days per week, sets, and resistance, but the progression is one in which you must listen to your body.

8.   Strength-training sessions are recommended to last one hour or less.

9.   As a general rule, each muscle that you train should be rested one to two days before being exercised further in order for the fatigued muscles to rebuild.

10.  "No pain, no gain." This statement is not only false, but it can also be dangerous. Your body will adapt to strength training and will reduce in body soreness each time you work out.[6]

Strength training will enhance your aerobic workout and help you become toned and trim, lean and strong! There are many strength-training programs and guidelines available; you just need to make the commitment and do the research. As you get started in your strength-training program, it will be helpful for you to learn the names of the major muscle groups and know which strength-training exercises target each group. The following list will help you decide the exercises that will best help you.[7]

## MUSCLE GROUPS AND STRENGTH TRAINING

| The major muscle groups | Strength training exercises to use |
|---|---|
| Gluteals—includes the gluteus maximus, which is the big muscle covering your behind | Squats, leg press, and lunges |
| Quadriceps—muscles at the front of the thigh | Squats, lunges, and leg press |
| Hamstrings—muscles at the back of the thigh | Squats, lunges, leg press, and leg curl |
| Hip abductors—muscles of the outer thigh; and hip adductors—muscles of the inner thigh | Side-lying leg lifts, standing cable pulls, and multi-hip machines |
| Calf—muscles on the back or lower leg | Standing calf raises, seated or bent-knee calf raises |
| Low back—the erector spinae muscles that extend the back and aid in good posture | Back extension machine, prone back extension, squats, and dead lift |
| Abdominals—muscles running the length of the abdomen and down the sides and front of the abdomen | Crunches, curls, reverse curls, and reverse crunches (where the hips are lifted instead of the head and shoulders) |
| Pectoralis major—large fan-shaped muscle that covers the front of the upper chest | Push-ups, pull-ups, and regular and incline bench press |
| Rhomboids—muscles in the middle of the upper back between the shoulder blades | Chin-ups and dumbbell bent rows |
| Trapezius—upper portion of the back | Upright rows and shoulder shrugs with resistance |

### Muscle Groups and Strength Training

| *The major muscle groups* | *Strength training exercises to use* |
| --- | --- |
| Latisimus dorsi—large muscles of the mid-back | Pull-ups, chin-ups, one-arm bent rows, dips on parallel bars, and the lat pull-down machine |
| Deltoids—the cap of the shoulder | Push-ups, bench press, and dumbbell raises |
| Biceps—the front of the upper arm | Biceps curls, chin-ups, and upright rows |
| Triceps—back of the upper arm | Push-ups, dips, triceps extensions, triceps kick-backs, and overhead (French) presses |

When you begin your exercise program, you are likely to experience some muscle soreness. Do not be discouraged, for you are using muscles that need to be strengthened. Be careful not to overexercise when you begin, and always precede your strength-training exercise with the proper stretching exercises to get you ready.

### FLEXIBILITY STRETCHING

Stretching for flexibility is a complement and preparation to your cardiovascular program of exercise. Stretching helps to lengthen all of your muscles, builds strong bones and balance, and helps you to breathe deeply. Stretching after an exercise program helps to calm and relax you. An exercise program that focuses on stretching and strengthening your muscles and joints is Pilates. It is recommended that you do Pilates three times a week.

A complete stretching routine can take as little as ten minutes. The best time to stretch is after you have warmed up and the muscles are warm. The best time to perform your flexibility routine is after exercise. This is when the muscles are the warmest and when you can use the relaxation. Focus on stretching the muscles you use the most during your specific exercise or sport.[8]

Be sure that you use proper technique when doing your stretching. Remember to stretch the muscles on both sides of your body. Never stretch to the point of pain or discomfort. Go slow! Always stretch slowly and evenly. Hold the stretch for about fifteen seconds, and release slowly as well. Do not bounce or jerk while stretching. This can cause injury as a muscle is pushed beyond its ability. And don't forget to breathe.[9]

> *Dr. Janet's Recommendation:*
>
> When added to your bath water, Epsom salt or sea salts contain ingredients that, when absorbed by the body, have anti-inflammatory action.

The following chart will give you some recommended stretches to use in your flexibility stretching.

### FLEXIBILITY STRETCHING

- *Hamstrings:* Sit on the floor with one leg straight in front of you and the other leg bent (with the sole of the foot touching the inside thigh of the outstretched leg). Keep your back straight, and lean forward from the hips. Slide your arms forward toward your outstretched foot. Stop when you feel a pull in the hamstring. Hold for fifteen seconds, and then repeat with the other leg extended.

- *Hips:* Lie on your back. Bend your left leg and bring it toward you. Grasp your left knee gently with your right hand and pull it slightly down and to the right until you feel a stretch. Turn your head to the left. Your right leg should stay flat on the floor. Hold for ten seconds, and then repeat with the other leg.

- *Low back:* Lie flat on the floor with knees bent. Use

your hands to pull your knees toward your chest. Lift your head and shoulders off the floor until your head is approximately 6 inches from your knees. Cross your ankles. Gently rock yourself back and forth in this position for thirty seconds.

- ➣ *Quadriceps*: Lie on your right side with your right knee bent at a 90-degree angle. Bend your left leg, and hold on to the ankle with your left hand. Gently pull your left heel in toward the left side of your butt. As soon as you feel a stretch in your left quad, slowly lower your left knee toward the floor behind your right knee. Hold for fifteen seconds, and then repeat with the other leg.

- ➣ *Calves*: Stand an arm's length away from a wall with your feet shoulder-width apart. Slide the left foot back approximately 18 inches, keeping the knee straight and both heels flat on the floor. Bend your right knee, and slowly move your pelvis forward until you feel a stretch in the calf and Achilles of the left leg. Hold for fifteen seconds, and then repeat with the other leg.[10]

## DEVELOP YOUR OWN EXERCISE PROGRAM

I want you to build your own exercise program. Make it one that you can stick with. Remember, exercise improves just about everything! It improves the functional capability of your organs, improves circulation, loosens and limbers up your joints and muscles, reduces stress, releases endorphins, reduces insomnia, and works off nervous energy.

> "A quick thirty-minute workout is better than nothing."
> —JORGE CRUISE, *FITSMART*

You may want to try the following ten-minute workout to get you going. Most women can find ten minutes of time in their day to concentrate on balancing their bodies. This workout will help you to experience the benefits of exercise and will give you the motivation to focus on each of the three areas of exercise we have covered in this chapter.

## No Time to Exercise?
## Try This Ten-Minute Workout

*One-leg lunges*

Stand with your back to your bed, and place your right foot on it. Hold on to something sturdy for support. Slowly lower yourself by bending your left knee. Make sure you can always see your left toes. If you can't, move forward so that your knee stays behind your toes when you bend. Hold; then slowly come back up. Repeat with the right leg.

*Push-ups*

Lie on your stomach on top of a towel or blanket with your knees bent, ankles crossed, and hands by your shoulders. As you press into the floor and straighten your arms, slowly lift your chest, hips, and thighs. Hold; then slowly lower. Before you touch the floor, push up again.

*Back extensions*

Lying on your stomach, place your hands under your chin. Keeping your feet on the floor, slowly lift your head and chest about three to five inches. Hold; then slowly lower.

*Crunches*

Lie on your back with your knees bent, feet flat on the floor, and hands behind your head. Pressing your lower back to the floor, slowly lift your head, shoulders, and upper back. Hold; then slowly lower.

*Chair-ups*

Sitting on the edge of a chair, place your hands on the edge by your butt. (Make sure the chair is stable and won't slide out from

under you.) Move your feet a few steps forward so that your butt is off the chair and your knees are bent at 90-degree angles. Bending your elbows so they point behind you, lower yourself as far as comfortable. Hold; then slowly press back up.

*Triceps extensions*
With a towel around your neck, drape a resistance band over the back of your neck and bend your arms to hold the band near your chest. Keeping your elbows at your sides, straighten your arms. Hold; then slowly release.

*Lateral raises*
Sitting on a chair, place the end of a resistance band under or around your right foot, and hold the other end in your right hand with your arm down at your side. Keeping a slight bend in your elbow, slowly lift your right arm out to your side until it's about shoulder height. Hold; then slowly lower. Repeat with the left arm.

*Biceps curls*
Sit on a chair with a resistance band under both feet. With your elbows at your sides, bring your hands, holding the resistance band, toward your shoulders. Hold; then slowly lower.

*Seated rows*
Sit on the floor with your back straight and legs out in front, knees slightly bent. Loop a resistance band over your feet at the arches. Squeezing your shoulder blades, pull your arms (with your hands holding the resistance band) back toward your chest so that your elbows are pointing behind you. Hold; then slowly release.

Remember, the key is not to dive into an exercise program that will not fit your life. A fancy club membership and a home gym sound good, but will they do *you* any good? Start slow, make it enjoyable, and build upon it slowly. Once you hit upon what works for you, it will become a habit much like brushing your teeth.

Exercise has very real and proven benefits for your physical body. It also has profound and far-reaching positive effects on your healing and balance, emotionally and spiritually.

Exercise not only improves the condition of your physical frame, but it also provides similar improvements in depression as antidepressant medication. This may be because women feel better and are more confident when they are stronger, or it may be due to the fact that exercise produces a positive biochemical change in the brain. It is probably a combination of both. Exercise provides a boost in self-esteem and self-confidence, and it has an enormous impact on your overall quality of life. This, in turn, will lift your spirits.

On page 132 is a protocol that will help alleviate muscle pain naturally. But because arthritis limits so many women from following an exercise program, I have designed the following protocol to help alleviate arthritis pain naturally.

## 🍃 *Dr. Janet's Protocol for Arthritis Pain*

### NATURAL SUPPORT FOR PAIN

- Glucosamine, 1,500 mg
- Boswellia, 150 mg three times daily
- Bromelain, 1,500 mg
- Magnesium, 800 mg daily
- Kava for stress relief
- White willow bark, nature's aspirin
- Passionflower, nature's sedative
- Black cohosh for neck pain
- Have a green drink daily
- For topical pain relief, use Dr. Janet's Glucosamine Cream, Chinese white flower oil, or castor oil packs.

## Dietary Support for Pain

- Eat foods low in fats and high in minerals with plenty of complex carbohydrates and vegetable protein like brown rice, broccoli, peas, seafood, tofu, and miso.
- Cherries, berries, and pineapple are nature's anti-inflammatories.
- Drink eight glasses of water each day (dehydration worsens pain).
- Avoid diuretics like caffeine, teas, and coffee.
- Avoid acid-producing foods like red meat, sugar, and salty foods.
- Use massage therapy and therapeutic baths.

CHAPTER 6

# SLEEP—THE PAUSE THAT REFRESHES

A good night's sleep is truly *the pause that refreshes*. Proper sleep is crucial for a woman's physical and mental health. In addition, when a woman is deprived of sleep, her immune system is weakened because the body's production of natural killer cells becomes impaired, thereby increasing the risk of illness and disease.

Sleep deprivation clouds your thoughts, changes your personality, and ages you faster than time itself. It is one of the most powerful midlife rejuvenators and costs you nothing. Many women would pay just about anything for a night of sweet, sound sleep. In women, sleep is elusive for a number of reasons.

## SLEEP DEPRIVERS

- Hormonal changes at menopause
- Hot flashes
- Night sweats
- Anxiety
- Depression
- Illness
- Chronic pain

Whatever the cause for sleep deprivation, it is vital to our well-being to sleep soundly. It is only during rest that the bone marrow and lymph nodes produce substances to empower our immune systems. Furthermore, it is during the beginning of our sleep cycle that much of the body's repair work is done.

Are you getting enough sleep? With our busy schedules and life-styles, most women today do not get enough recuperative sleep to maintain good balance physically, emotionally, and spiritually. Take the following test to see if you are experiencing excessive daytime sleepiness as a result of less than adequate nighttime sleep.

### Epworth Sleepiness Scale

In contrast to just feeling tired, how likely are you to doze off or fall asleep in the following situations? (Even if you have not done some of these things recently, try to work out how they would have affected you.) Use the following scale to choose the most appropriate number for each situation.

0 = Would never doze
1 = Slight chance of dozing
2 = Moderate chance of dozing
3 = High chance of dozing

| Chance of Dozing | Situation |
| --- | --- |
| _____ | Sitting and reading |
| _____ | Watching TV |
| _____ | Sitting inactive in a public place (i.e., theater) |
| _____ | As a car passenger for an hour with no break |
| _____ | Lying down to rest in the afternoon |
| _____ | Sitting and talking to someone |
| _____ | Sitting quietly after lunch without alcohol |

———————   In a car, while stopping for a few minutes in
traffic

A score greater than 10 is a definite cause for concern as it indicates significant excessive daytime sleepiness.[1]

Many midlife women tell me that they would love to be able to sleep as soundly as they did before they had children. Declining hormonal levels may be responsible as well as the fact that motherhood conditioned us to become *light sleepers*. As children become teens, mothers often keep an *all-night vigil*, waiting for teens to return home safe and sound from their evening escapades. Often, it's well after midnight, which leaves only a few hours until dawn to drift off to dream land.

## A *hidden cause of fatigue*

If you suffer from fatigue, you may have an iodine deficiency. A lack of iodine can impair your thyroid function, and a sluggish thyroid can leave you feeling tired and weak.

Luckily, there's an excellent test you can do at home to check your iodine levels. Simply take a Q-tip, dip it into a 2 percent tincture of iodine (available at any drugstore or supermarket), and paint a 2-inch square on your thigh or belly. This will leave a yellowish stain that should disappear in about twenty-four hours if your iodine levels are normal.

If the stain disappears in less than twenty-four hours, it means your body is deficient in iodine and has thirstily sucked it up. If that's the case, keep applying the iodine every day at different sites until the stain lasts a full twenty-four hours.

Not only will you have diagnosed your iodine deficiency, but you will also have treated that deficiency and improved your thyroid function! Have your thyroid levels checked to determine if you are suffering from poor thyroid function. It is important for you to address your thyroid health!

## Symptoms of Sleep Deprivation

Common symptoms of sleep deprivation include:

- Tiredness
- Irritability, edginess
- Inability to tolerate stress
- Problems with concentration and memory
- Behavioral, learning, or social problems
- Frequent infections
- Blurred vision
- Vague discomfort
- Alterations in appetite
- Activity intolerance

It must be noted that many of these symptoms can be related to disabling conditions. This overlap of symptoms may make it difficult to determine if they are caused by sleep deprivation or the disability.

Some suggestions to help you determine the cause of your sleep deprivation include talking to your health-care provider and keeping a log that contains signs and symptoms, situations affecting your sleep, medications, diet, and so forth. Remember to take the log with you when you discuss your sleep problems with your health-care provider.[2]

Other causes of sleeplessness include the use of decongestant medications, cold remedies, antibiotics, appetite suppressants, contraceptives, and thyroid medications. Sleep is a supreme tonic. It is important that you take steps to sleep deeply and restoratively. You need to determine and change the cause of your insomnia. If you are taking prescription sleep aids, you should know that sleeping pills impair calcium absorption, are habit forming, and paralyze the part of your brain that controls dreaming. Many times they can leave us feeling less than rested and impair clarity of thought.

Dramatic facts related to sleep deprivation are slowly coming to light. Each year sleep disorders add $16 billion to national health-care costs (for example, by contributing to high blood pressure and heart disease), not including accidents and lost productivity at work. The National Commission on Sleep Disorders has estimated that sleep deprivation costs $150 billion a year in higher stress and reduced workplace productivity. Major industrial disasters have been attributed to sleep deprivation (among these, at least in part, Three Mile Island, Chernobyl, the gas leak at Bhopal, the Zeebrugge ferry disaster, and the Exxon Valdez oil spill).[3]

There is much evidence to help us understand that a lack of sleep impairs our performance during our waking hours. Science has indicated that it is necessary for optimum health to get at least eight hours of sleep *every night*. Yet because of our busy lifestyles, we often find ourselves burning the candle at both ends, staying up late and getting up early in the morning.

Take a look at the following chart, which lists some of the evidences of impaired performance due to sleep deprivation that researchers have found.

### LACK OF SLEEP IMPAIRS PERFORMANCE

Let's say that a person who needs eight hours of sleep per night only gets six. This two-hour sleep loss can have a major impact, including:

- Reduced alertness
- Shortened attention span
- Slower than normal reaction time
- Poorer judgment
- Reduced awareness of the environment and situation
- Reduced decision-making skills

- Poorer memory
- Reduced concentration
- Increased likelihood of mentally "stalling" or fixating on one thought
- Increased likelihood of moodiness and bad temper
- Reduced work efficiency
- Loss of motivation
- Errors of omission (making a mistake by forgetting to do something)
- Errors of commission (making a mistake by doing something but choosing the wrong option)
- Microsleep (brief periods of involuntary sleeping that range from a few seconds to a few minutes in duration)[4]

While trying to reestablish a healthy sleep pattern, there are a few rules. Avoid caffeinated foods and drinks such as coffee, teas, sodas, and chocolate. You should also avoid late-night eating. It has been said, "Sleep doesn't interfere with digestion, but digestion interferes with sleep." If you do eat late, choose a food that will promote relaxation like plain yogurt or turkey, which are rich in sleep-inducing tryptophan; oatmeal, which tends to promote sleep; bananas; tuna; whole-grain crackers; or maybe a cup of chamomile tea, which is considered to be a nerve restorative and helps quiet anxiety and stress. This is probably due to the fact that it is high in magnesium, calcium, potassium, and B vitamins. Other natural sleep aids include:

*Dr. Janet's Recommendation:*

If you want to live a balanced life, you must work to reestablish good sleep habits in your life.

- *Passionflower*—helps to relax the mind and muscles. A non-drowsy sleep aid, it is an antispasmodic and sedative.

Take 30 drops (tincture) or 500-mg capsule one-half hour before bed.

- *Skullcap*—considered one of the best tonics for the nervous system.
- *Valerian\**—helps anxiety-related sleep disorders.[5] Take valerian thirty to sixty minutes before bed, using 30–60 drops of tincture or 300–500 mg capsule or tablet. Valerian has a strong odor that many people object to, so it is not usually desired as a tea by most people. Some people may feel groggy or experience a "hangover effect" from valerian. If so, passionflower may be a better choice to help improve your sleep.

   \*WARNING: Do not combine valerian or passionflower with tranquilizers or antidepressant medications. If you are taking these medications, be sure to talk to your health-care provider before you take any dose of valerian.
- *Hops*—helps to induce sleep and is a safe and reliable sedative.
- *Melatonin*—a natural hormone that promotes sound sleep.
- *DHEA*—a natural hormone that improves the quality of sleep.
- *L-theanine*—an amino acid taken thirty minutes before bed that promotes deep muscle relaxation.
- *Calcium*—has a calming effect and with magnesium feeds the nerves.
- *Magnesium*—relaxes muscles and with calcium feeds the nerves.
- *Inositol*—enhances REM sleep (rapid eye movement sleep), which means the stage of deep sleep where dreaming occurs.

Deficiencies in potassium and the B vitamins, so common in midlife due to stress or chronic pain syndromes, may also be a factor in the poor sleep picture. Lack of sleep robs your body of essential

downtime necessary to rebuild vital organs and recharge your nervous system. Anyone who has just returned from a restful vacation can attest that they feel rejuvenated. Friends and co-workers will usually comment on how rested and relaxed they appear. Just think…if it is so evident on the outside, imagine what has taken place inside the body, mind, and spirit. Sleep—it's a good thing!

Sleep experts state that some women thrive on four hours of sleep a night, while others need at least ten to feel rested. In order to find out what is right for you, go to bed when you are tired and get up when you wake up for a week, and calculate how long you spent in bed. Divide the week's total by seven—that is your optimal "sleep number."

### Dr. Janet's Sleep Cocktail

½ cup grape juice

½ cup water

1–2 capsules of L-theanine

1–2 capsules Slow Mag (magnesium chloride)

10 drops passionflower extract

Combine all ingredients, and drink thirty minutes before bed.

### GOOD SLEEP HABITS

The following tips about sleeping make sense for all ages:

- Go to bed and awake at the same time each day, even on weekends.
- There is no way to make up for *lost sleep*.
- Establish a daily *cool-down* time. One hour before bedtime, dim the lights and eliminate noise. Use this time for low-level stimulation activities such as listening to quiet music or reading nonstimulating material.

- Associate your bed with resting. Talk on the phone or surf the Internet elsewhere.
- Don't drink caffeinated drinks in the afternoon or evening. Caffeine's stimulating effects will peak two to four hours after consumption, but they can linger in the body for several hours.
- Don't eat dinner close to bedtime, and don't allow overeating. Sleep can be disrupted by digestive systems working extra hard after a heavy meal.
- Avoid exercise close to bedtime. Physical activity late in the day can affect your body's ability to relax into a peaceful slumber.[6]

# CHAPTER 7

# TRUE BEAUTY—NATURALLY

Beauty truly does radiate from within. A healthy, vibrant woman defies age. As a testimony and reflection of our self-esteem, inner beauty, and vibrancy, true beauty is the result of inner vitality, balance, health, and happiness. Optimal nutrition, stress-relieving exercise, and a positive frame of mind are requirements you must tote along on your continued journey toward complete balance. A balanced body and a beautiful spirit are better than the very best cosmetic application or surgery.

With proper nutrition, rest, relaxation, and exercise, you can keep your body in balance, healthy, and youthful throughout your entire life. Your skin can be wrinkle free and elastic, your eyes can sparkle, your complexion can be smooth, and your face can be firm and tight. Many famous women in history were known for their beauty well into old age. They realized how uplifting it was, not only to themselves but also for those around them, to methodically work on achieving vibrant health and beauty at any age. They frequently used natural beauty aids, exotic oils, facials, and aromatic baths. They did not overeat, they did not smoke, and they avoided alcohol and excessive sun exposure. They knew that it was important to address constipation immediately with herbs or fiber to help eliminate poisons or toxins from their bodies as quickly as possible.

In this chapter I will offer you the latest discoveries from the world of nutrition that have been shown to have antiaging properties. I will also outline many of the very latest beauty treatments that women of today partake of on a regular basis. When it comes to aging, there are two choices: you either *embrace it*, or you try to *erase it* with cosmetic procedures and injectable fillers.

## LET'S BEGIN WITH SKIN SINS

### Smoking

Smoking is the most damaging thing you can do to your skin, second only to sun exposure. The nicotine found in cigarettes constricts the blood vessels in your face, making your skin look gray or sallow. Then add in acetaldehyde, which attacks the fibers in your skin that hold it together. Finally, a chemical reaction occurs, creating a protein that causes the destruction of collagen and elastin. Factor in the constant creasing and wrinkling of the eyes due to smoke irritation and the pursing of your lips, and you have all the ingredients for looking ten years older than women who do not smoke!

The good news is that quitting before the age of thirty returns your body to the level of a nonsmoker within ten years—and that includes your skin, too! Smoking uses up tissue oxygen, which feeds the brain and helps prevent disease. Each cigarette takes eight minutes off your life; one pack a day takes one month off of your life each year, and two packs take ten to twelve years off your life. In addition, cigarettes have over four thousand known poisons.[1] You'll be interested to know that just one drop of nicotinic acid can kill a man.[2]

### Sun

Nothing ages you faster and damages collagen and elastin more rapidly (in three minutes in peak sunlight!) than sun exposure. The good news here is that you can prevent sun damage by wearing sunscreen whenever you leave the house. You should wear at least SPF-15. Wear SPF-30 if you are a golfer or if you spend time at the beach. Sunscreen not only protects you from future sun damage, but it can also help actually reverse past damage because, with protection, your skin gets a chance to repair itself. Stay covered or out of the sun completely if possible between the hours of 11:00 a.m. and 3:00 p.m.

## Alcohol

Alcohol dilates blood vessels, leading to broken veins. Like cigarettes, alcohol also contains acetaldehyde, which attacks skin fibers and reduces elasticity and firmness. In addition, alcohol robs the body of vitamin C, a key nutrient for healthy skin.

## Lack of sleep

I consider sleep to be the best *beauty vitamin* in the entire world. Nighttime is when your body repairs itself. This includes your skin. Collagen and elastin are replaced and new cells are built, thereby erasing the previous day's exposure to sun and environmental toxins. Your skin is more absorbent and receptive at night, so it is a perfect time to moisturize and add topical vitamin treatments. Lack of sleep will cut these benefits, leaving you with dark circles, puffiness, sallowness, and even pimples.

## Stress

Stress increases the levels of adrenal hormones, like testosterone, which can trigger acne. Stress hormones can also cause your blood flow to be directed away from your limbs and major organs, leaving your skin crying out for the nutrients it needs. When you are stressed, it is harder to repair your complexion with skin care. Stressed skin simply does not respond to or absorb skin treatments as well as relaxed skin. Practice deep breathing and diaphragmatic breathing, exercise, and/or take a tub bath with lavender essential oil to help de-stress your body, mind, and spirit.

## Lack of exercise

Exercise boosts oxygen in your blood and in turn improves your skin tone. Exercise, as I have mentioned before, increases your tolerance to stress and helps you sleep, which will boost your skin health as well. For optimal skin health, try to do three sets of twenty minutes

of exercise each week. Try cycling, walking at a good pace, swimming, and running, if your joints are healthy.

*Caffeine*

Every cup of coffee you drink needs three cups of water to process it through the system. It is very dehydrating to the skin. In addition, caffeine increases your level of stress hormones, which, as I discussed, can lead to poor skin health.

## SKIN CARE

In today's world, the skin care and cosmetic surgery industry is booming and has become one of the largest, most profitable industries in America. Like women before us, we are on a constant search for the latest and greatest botanical, liposomal, antioxidant, exfoliant, or hydrator in the world to make us appear more beautiful with skin that is visibly younger and smoother.

The fact remains that even in our advanced generation, beautiful skin is so much more than skin deep. Yes, there are lunchtime peels, microdermabrasion, laser resurfacing, and other techniques to smooth and erase fine lines, but it is an undeniable fact that beautiful skin is still the result of a healthy, toxin-free body.

There are many factors that come into play in regard to great skin. Why is it that some women can go to the corner drugstore and use any low-priced moisturizer that may be on sale that week and have wonderful skin complete with luminosity, velvety texture and perfect tone, while others travel to major department stores to purchase only the highest-quality skin-care products with a price tag to match and still be dissatisfied with their complexion?

The answer is simple, yet complex, in terms of all of the systems of the body that play a role in beautiful skin. The skin is the largest organ of the body, and it receives great benefit from an enzyme-rich circulatory system. Skin that is well enriched by oxygen and high-quality nutrients will always look smooth, firm, and velvety.

Enzymes are the digestive catalysts that make nutrients available to the blood for their journey to every cell in the body. To feed, detoxify, slow the aging process, oxygenate, and boost the circulatory system, you must make midlife enzyme supplementation a priority. Skin needs constant and continuous nutrition from within that only enzymes can supply. Once an enzyme program has been implemented, many women notice that long-standing skin conditions begin to clear up after just fourteen days into enzyme therapy.

The goal for the digestive enzymes you use with each meal is to be sure they come from a plant source. The formula should contain the following: amylase, lipase, protease, cellulase, lactase, maltase, and sucrase. And it should be taken with meals or between meals. There are several skin-beautifying enzymes, including:

- *Protease*: breaks down protein foods that feed the cells of the dermis; also improves distribution of all nutrients to the skin
- *Amylase*: reduces skin inflammation
- *Lipase*: keeps skin cells plump to reduce wrinkling
- *Cellulase*: breaks down fiber and allows nutrients access to the skin

When we are young, our skin is soft, supple, and glowing. Beautiful skin comes naturally in our youth. But as we age, beautiful skin is a reward for taking proper care of our bodies. The skin is a barometer that reflects what is going on with us internally. Skin care is big business these days as baby boomers anxiously take part in staving off the signs of aging. Stress, excessive sun exposure, liver malfunction, hormone depletion, smoking, alcohol, sugar, fried foods, caffeine, and poor circulation all contribute to the condition of our skin. Age spots, wrinkles, dry skin, uneven skin tone, sallow complexion, and acne are the result of how well our systems handle wastes. Free-radical damage is a major contributor to poor skin.

For healthy, glowing skin, begin to do some simple things that will greatly benefit your skin.

### Skin Care Dietary Therapy

- Drink plenty of water, eight to ten glasses each day.
- Add fresh lemon for added benefit.
- Make a fresh "liver cocktail" each day (use a juicer). The juice consists of 2 ounces beet juice, 3 ounces of carrot juice, and 3 ounces of cucumber juice.
- Avoid sugars, caffeine, and red meat to prevent dehydration.
- Eat fresh fruit and vegetables each day; fruits are wonderful cleaners.

### Body Therapy

- Reduce or prevent wrinkles by rubbing papaya skins on the face. (Papain is an enzyme that exfoliates the skin.)
- Manage stress.
- Practice deep breathing.
- Have a massage with almond oil, sesame oil, or wheat germ oil to soften the skin.
- Moisturize immediately after bathing.
- Rub lemon juice on age spots or use 2 percent hydroquinone topical cream to reduce and fade age spots.
- Limit sun exposure: always use a sunblock SPF-15 or more to prevent further damage and to prevent age spots from darkening.

### Beauty Big Three

- Detoxify and eat healthy.
- Moisturize and drink plenty of water.
- Protect by using sunscreen; limit sun exposure.

## BEAUTY BENEFITS FROM NATURE

Watermelon juice is rich in natural silica, which supports collagen and reduces wrinkled and dry skin. The condition of your skin can be the first thing to alert you that you need to start a detoxification program. If your colon becomes stagnant with toxins and your liver does not filter wastes and impurities coming from the digestive tract, your skin will give you a sure sign—rashes, acne, boils, blotchiness, uneven skin tone, dermatitis, and itchy skin. After detoxification, your skin will glow and your skin problems will diminish or disappear.

Below I have listed some additional dietary recommendations from nature's bounty that will help encourage glowing skin:

### DIETARY BENEFITS FOR BEAUTIFUL SKIN

- *Broccoli* is a good source of fiber, vitamin K, lutein, vitamin C, calcium, and folate. It increases cell turnover of the skin and protects against environmental damage.
- *Walnuts* are a source of omega-3 fatty acids, vitamin E, protein, fiber, magnesium, polyphenols, and vitamin $B_6$. They protect skin from UV damage.
- *Spinach* is a source of omega-3 fatty acids, beta-carotene, B vitamins, polyphenols, and alpha lipoic acid. It helps to reduce wrinkles and the chemical levels associated with the aging process. It increases cell turnover and protects against environmental damage.
- *Oranges* are a source of vitamin C, fiber, folate, potassium, polyphenols, and pectin. They reduce environmental effects on the skin.
- *Salmon* is a source of omega-3 fatty acids, B vitamins, selenium, potassium, protein, and vitamin D. It helps to reduce wrinkles and chemical levels associated

with the aging process. It can help reduce the severity of acne breakouts. It increases the strength of hair and encourages hair growth.

- *Green tea* is a source of flavonoids and fluoride. It helps to reduce cellular inflammation associated with aging.
- *Blueberries* are a source of carotenoids, vitamins C and E, iron, niacin, polyphenols, and phytonutrients. They increase hair root health through improved circulation and reduce the environmental effects on the skin.
- *Pumpkin* is a source of vitamins C and E, beta-carotene, fiber, potassium, and magnesium. It protects the skin against environmental damage and increases cell turnover.
- *Shellfish* are great sources of iodine, which supports your thyroid gland health. They include lobster, shrimp, scallops, mussels, and clams.

## Skin-Beautifying Nutrients

- *Vitamin C*: Feeds collagen, which is one of the most important substances in the structure of the skin. Sources include kiwifruit, oranges, red peppers, blueberries, and melon.
- *Vitamin A and/or beta-carotene*: A powerful antioxidant that helps your skin produce keratin and proteins that help with cell regeneration. Sources include carrots, peaches, pumpkin, and sweet potatoes.
- *Vitamin E*: Antioxidant that promotes scar healing and combats the signs of aging.
- *Zinc*: Vital for skin healing. It reduces acne. Sources include nuts, seeds, and hard crumbly cheeses.
- *Iron*: Low levels can mean pale skin and dark circles.

This may also be indicative of anemia. Check with your doctor. If your iron level is low, include dark leafy vegetables in your diet, lean red meat, and a green drink each day.[3]

- *Gingko biloba*: To increase circulation
- *ACES*: For free-radical damage—vitamins A, C, E, and selenium
- *CoQ$_{10}$*: 100 mg daily
- *Evening primrose oil*
- *DMAE (dimethylaminoethanol)*: An amino acid that prevents sagging skin and increases skin's firmness.
- *Idebenone*: This is a power antioxidant that protects your skin from free-radical damage, thereby reducing fine lines and wrinkles and evening out your complexion.
- *Kinetin*: A naturally occurring compound that fends off free radicals. It reduces wrinkles and retains the skin's moisture. Kinetin is nonirritating and has anti-inflammatory properties.
- *Alpha lipoic acid*: External application of this powerful antioxidant helps protect genetic material, such as DNA, in the body, which can reduce the effect of aging.
- *Alpha hydroxy acids (fruit acid)*: To exfoliate the skin
- *Dr. Janet's Woman's Balance Progesterone Formula*: Available from www.DrJanetPhD.com
- *Water*: Keeps your cells plump and promotes a healthy glow. Drink eight glasses per day. Make one glass per hour your goal, and add fresh lemon for extra benefit.
- Whole-body herbal cleansing formula

*Avoid eye infections*

There are some cautions you should take to avoid a sty, which is a painful, pus-filled infection of the eyelid. Sties are caused by allergy or viral or bacterial infections. *Do not sleep with your eye makeup on!* This can contribute to bacterial eye infections. Make sure to discard old mascara, eyeliner, and eye shadow that is more than six months old. Never squeeze a sty. It can cause the infection to spread.

## BATHS

There are soothing, therapeutic baths that will aid in both helping your physical body to look and feel better externally and in purifying the toxins and impurities within your body. These can be very soothing and relaxing, and could become a part of your regular *beauty* regime.

I am going to suggest two types of baths in this section. The first are baths using aromatherapy, which will aid in your emotional balance, providing you with fresh energy, an attitude check, and a new outlook on life.

*Aromatherapy baths*

Some aromatherapy essences are stronger than others and are used for different effects, so count out just a few drops of some common scents and get revitalized. If you are just beginning aromatherapy, I recommend you choose one or two of the following essential oils to put in your bath.

1. *Restful bath*: For maximum relaxation, I suggest you add to a tubful of water one of these essential oils: chamomile (two drops), cypress (five drops), orange blossom (two drops), or lavender (six drops).
2. *No-more blahs bath*: Try lemon (four drops), peppermint (four drops), basil (three drops), or bergamot (three drops).
3. *Spicy bath*: Feel fresh with geranium (three drops), lavender (six drops), juniper (five drops), or cardamom (four drops).

4. *Wake-up bath*: For a stimulating bath, use basil (three drops), peppermint (four drops), juniper (five drops), hyssop (three drops), or rosemary (five drops).

5. *Tension bath*: Ease your way through the end of the week with bergamot (three drops), juniper (five drops), hyssop (three drops), or rosemary (five drops).[4]

*Purification baths*

When you are following the healthy guidelines in this book for ridding your body of imbalance and learning to live in balance—physically, emotionally, and spiritually, you may experience flu-like symptoms during the detoxification because your body is ridding itself of poisons. You can get relief from these symptoms by taking baths using Epsom salts (1 to 2 cups) and baking soda (1 cup) in a tub of water. Soak for twenty minutes (longer than twenty minutes may be too exhausting). On off days, you can put 1 cup of apple cider vinegar in the tub and soak.

> *Dr. Janet's Recommendation:*
>
> Back and shoulder aches are a common part of a woman's everyday life—heal these complaints in the bath!

Skin brushing can be very beneficial, because the skin is a primary avenue for detoxification along with the lungs, kidneys, liver, and colon. Use a vegetable brush. You can purchase this at a health food store. You need to brush all parts of the body toward the heart. Then follow with a sesame oil massage. Massaging with sesame oil brings relief. This oil can also be purchased from a health food store. Massage the whole body for five minutes before bathing or showering.

Or choose one of these purifying baths to help you find balance in your life.

1. *Clorox bath*: This is to help remove heavy metals from the body and add oxygen. Use ½ cup of Clorox brand bleach (*only* this brand) to a tub of warm water. Soak for twenty-five minutes. You can shower off with soap and fresh water

afterward, but it is not necessary. If your skin feels a bit itchy, this will relieve it.

2. *Epsom salts and ginger*: This bath opens pores, eliminates toxins, and also helps to eliminate pain. Stir in 1 cup Epsom salts and 2 tablespoons of ginger in 1 cup of water first, then add it to the bath. Do not remain in the tub for more than thirty minutes.

3. *Salt and soda*: This bath also counteracts the affects of radiation, whether from X-rays, cancer treatment radiation, fallout from the atmosphere, or television radiation. Add 1 cup of baking soda and 1–2 cups of ordinary coarse salt, Epsom salts, or sea salt to a tub of water. You can soak for twenty minutes.

4. *Epsom salts, sea salt, and oil*: This bath helps with dry skin and stress. Add 1 cup of Epsom salts, 1 cup of sea salt (from health food store), and 1 cup of sesame oil to a warm to hot tub of water, and soak for twenty minutes. Pat yourself dry.

5. *Vinegar bath*: This is used when the body is too acidic and is a quick way of restoring the acid-alkaline balance. Add 1 cup to 2 quarts of 100 percent apple cider vinegar to a bathtub of warm water. Soak forty to forty-five minutes. This is excellent for excess uric acid in the body (especially in the joints), arthritis, bursitis, tendonitis, and gout.

6. *Bentonite bath*: This is a fast detoxification method. Soak 2–4 pounds of bentonite clay in a flat container overnight to dissolve it. Then add this to the tub of water. With 2 pounds of bentonite you would soak one hour; with 4 pounds, you would soak only about thirty minutes. The more bentonite used, the faster the detoxification.[5]

## Dr. Janet's Protocol for a Natural Spa Day

### HAVE A SPA DAY, NATURALLY!

*Moisturizing body treatment:*

- 1 avocado, mashed
- 1 cup oatmeal
- ½ cup finely ground almonds

Rub the mixture into the body, leave for five minutes, shower off, and then have a beauty bath.

*Beauty bath, a rich, moisturizing bath:*

- 1 cup oatmeal
- 3 cups powdered milk
- 1 muslin bag

Put oatmeal and powdered milk into the muslin bag. Tie it under the bath faucet and run the water through it.

> **Dr. Janet's Recommendation:**
>
> Two cups of milk or cream added to your bath will hydrate your skin.

*Super scrub, for sun-damaged skin:*

This super body scrub contains fruit acids that help dissolve dead skin cells that can be washed away.

- 1 guava
- 1 kiwifruit
- Handful of Dead Sea salts
- 2 Tbsp. honey

Apply to the body in circular motions; then rinse off.[6]

### BEAUTY THROUGH THE DECADES

There are some quick and minimally invasive skin therapies that can be recommended for the woman who desires to achieve better balance and lasting beauty decade by decade.

Are you in your twenties? Try the *Ellen Lange Retexurizing Peel Kit*. It contains alpha and beta hydroxy acids. Their exfoliating properties

keep your skin smooth and line free. It is available at Sephora.com at a cost of approximately $72.

Have you reached your thirties? Regular microdermabrasion sessions help keep superficial lines to a minimum. Alpha hydroxy acids (AHA) or beta hydroxy acids (BHA) smooth out fine wrinkles and brighten dull skin. These take ten to fifteen minutes in the office of a dermatologist or plastic surgeon. These sessions have become known as "lunch hour" peels and cost approximately $100–$150. Other microdermabrasion treatments may cost approximately $150 per session.

For those of you who have entered your forties, you might want to consider moving up to the TCA peel, which targets more pronounced wrinkles. Some dermatologists recommend that you have a series of peels spaced a month or two apart, each costing approximately $300.[7]

## THE SEARCH FOR TRUE BEAUTY

True beauty comes from the *inner woman*—her essence, her spirit. A truly beautiful woman is comprised of many attributes that work in symphony to produce a radiance that cannot be duplicated by the most skilled plastic surgeon or the most expensive topical beauty serum.

*Dr. Janet's Recommendation:*

A woman's reproductive hormones are boosted by sunlight. You should get at least thirty minutes of sunlight each day. For the most benefits, do this before 10:00 a.m. and after 2:00 p.m. when the UV rays are least intense.

While our society places great emphasis on physical beauty, and billions of dollars are spent on the pursuit of the latest beauty fads, fillers, injections, and trends, it is the *inner woman* that must radiate in order for a woman to be considered truly beautiful.

People naturally gravitate toward beauty. Think of nature—how we all reach out and are drawn to pick a beautiful flower, or to at least pause to smell and admire the beauty of a fragrant rose. We are drawn because we instinctively know that flowers are beautiful inside and out. We pick them not only for their visual beauty, but also for their sweet essence. And so it goes for women. True beauty comes from our very essence.

Beauty is in the eye of the beholder—when it comes to our physical appearance—but inner beauty speaks to everyone. The Bible even tells us to go beyond "outward adornment" and that beauty is "the hidden person of the heart" (1 Pet. 3:4, NKJV).

The most beautiful woman I have ever known had an essence that drew men and women alike with a power likened to Venus, the Greek goddess of love. Her outward appearance would never suggest that she had such magnetism. But, oh, how her essence captured the hearts of those around her. She was loyal, confident, strong, unselfish, dependable, unassuming, loving, a best friend, humorous, humble, and gentle. She gave of herself, never seeking approval. She had faith; she had worth; *she had beauty.*

The beauty guidelines I have given you in this chapter focus mainly on the outward appearance. You must remember that to experience beauty throughout your lifetime, you must cultivate it from within. Let it flow through you each day. Live a beautiful life—let beauty radiate from your body, your mind, and your spirit. Physical beauty is only skin deep and fades with the passing of time. True beauty comes from your core. Purpose to become *a rose in this garden of life.*

## AN ANTIAGING PROTOCOL

If you are a young or middle-aged woman, you can prevent many future problems by changing your habits now. If you are an older woman and are experiencing health issues, it is never too late to bring balance and harmony to your body. Aging is not a disease; it is a natural process. Most of the diseases that are normally associated with aging such as cancer, diabetes, digestive problems, depression, sexual dysfunction, and fatigue are not inevitable parts of growing older.

The late comedian George Burns, who lived to be one hundred, summed it up beautifully: "If I knew I was going to live this long, I would have taken better care of myself."

I believe that living to old age should be a blessing and not a curse. All of these *age-related* disorders are mainly caused by lifestyle factors such as poor diet, lack of exercise, and exposure to toxins, along with genetic susceptibilities.

Aging is accelerated by a lack of exercise. If you do not engage in regular exercise, you will increase your risk for almost every degenerative disease, including diabetes, osteoporosis, and heart disease. In addition, exercise helps to keep your blood sugar levels in the normal range.

The effects of stress play a role in the aging process as well. Women who endure long periods of intense stress are more likely to develop chronic disease. One of the biggest stressors for women is loneliness. One study found that lonely people have blood pressure readings that

BUILDING BLOCK 7

are as much as 30 points higher than people who are not lonely.[1] Nearly 60 percent of seniors ages fifty to sixty-eight were experiencing some form of loneliness.[2] Giving up or cutting back on social obligations, intellectual activities, sports, and exercise has been linked to a shorter life span and an increased risk of disease.

How can you know whether the signs of aging you are experiencing are occurring more quickly than they need to occur? Take the following quiz to help determine if you are aging faster than necessary.

### ANTIAGING SELF-EXAM

- ☐ Have you noticed brown spots on the back of your head or around your eyes and nose?
- ☐ Is it more difficult for you to lose weight?
- ☐ Do you have frequent indigestion, heartburn, or gas after eating a meal?
- ☐ Do you have insomnia?
- ☐ Do you have heart palpitations or chest pain?
- ☐ Do you have poor eyesight?
- ☐ Have you experienced hearing loss or ringing in the ears?
- ☐ Are you frequently constipated?
- ☐ Is your hair turning gray?
- ☐ Have you lost height?
- ☐ Is your skin becoming dryer or thinner? Are you noticing more moles, bruises, or cherry angiomas (red blood blisters)?
- ☐ Is your recovery time slow from a cold or flu?
- ☐ Do you have poor circulation?

## ATTITUDE AND AGING

All of us are getting older—and doing it much more quickly than any of us would like. However, researchers have discovered that our attitude plays a major role in how quickly we age. A study released in December 2005 suggests that the perceptions of senior citizens about the aging process depend not on disease or physical disability, but rather on attitude and coping style. "The medical community has not reached consensus on what constitutes successful aging," commented lead researcher Dilip Jeste, MD. "The commonly used criteria suggest that a person is aging well if they have a low level of disease and disability. However, this study shows that self-perception about aging can be more important than the traditional success markers."[3]

> You are only as old as you feel—take steps to feel great!

It is as important that you develop emotional balance about the prospect of growing older as it is that you know the latest physical protocols for slowing down the aging process. We will look closely at some of those tools for achieving physical balance about aging in this chapter. But it is just as important for you to learn to incorporate emotional tools to deal with the aging process.

Choose to be happy in your life—regardless of the circumstances or symptoms that seem negative. More and more studies are showing that we age better when we are happy and free of negative images of aging. One recent study found a link between positive emotions and the onset of frailty. The researchers speculate that positive emotions may directly affect health via chemical and neural responses involved in maintaining homeostatic balance.[4]

> Age is just a number!

Could it be that the poet Robert Browning was trying to encourage us all when he penned:

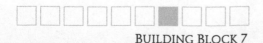

Grow old with me!
The best is yet to be.

## HEALTH SCREENINGS FOR EVERY WOMAN OVER FORTY

When it comes to your health care, you may have the impression that age forty marks the beginning of midlife meltdown. The fact is, prevention and early detection of disease should be the cornerstone of your midlife wellness plan. Think of it as a screening evolution that began with the very first vaccine you received as a newborn. You should consider having the following health screenings. Think of this as your "Balanced Woman Health Insurance Plan."

### Balanced Woman Health Insurance Plan

*Clinical Skin Exam*
Your doctor will do a head-to-toe skin check, looking for irregular moles and other signs of skin cancer. Women ages forty and older should have this test once a year.

*Colorectal Cancer Screenings*
Starting at age fifty, all adults should have a fecal occult blood test annually and a sigmoidoscopy every three to ten years to check for polyps or cancerous lesions. If you are at high risk for colorectal cancer, your physician may suggest a colonoscopy instead.

*Total Thyroxin Test (T4)*
This blood test assesses thyroid function. Talk to your physician about getting the test around menopause.

*Bone Density Test*
You'll need a baseline test at menopause to detect osteoporosis or assess your risk for the disease.

*Clinical Breast Exam*

Your physician should examine your breasts each year to look for lumps, swollen lymph nodes, and other irregularities.

*Mammogram*

A baseline mammogram is recommended by age forty, followed by mammograms every two years and annually after age fifty.

*Pap Smear*

You should have this test at least once every three years and annually if you are at high risk for cervical cancer. Yes, you need a Pap smear even if you have had a hysterectomy or are postmenopausal.

*Glaucoma Screening*

Get this eye test beginning at age forty. If you have normal vision, you should get an eye exam every three to five years.

*Electrocardiogram (ECG)*

You should get a baseline ECG by age forty. This painless test uses electrodes to record your heart's electrical impulses. The test evaluates heart function and can identify injury or abnormality.

*Blood Pressure Screening*

Blood pressure should be checked at least once every two years. If blood pressure is elevated, steps should be taken to control it; more frequent monitoring may be required.

*Cholesterol Test*

If your LDL, HDL, triglyceride, and total cholesterol levels fall within the desirable range, this simple blood test, which helps assess your risk of cardiovascular disease, should be performed every five years.[5]

Described here are general screening guidelines. Of course, every woman's needs are unique, so discuss your screening status with your

doctor. He or she may suggest additional tests or a different schedule. The goal is to support your body with system-specific nutrition, which will aid the healing process.

## OSTEOPOROSIS AND OSTEOMALACIA

For some people, the aging process brings an increase of muscle and joint pain and the onset of osteoporosis and osteomalacia. However, nature offers a bounty of protection and treatment of osteoporosis, which robs bones of their strength and density, and osteomalacia, which involves lowered calcium in the bone.

Take this quiz to see if you are at risk for these diseases:

- ☐ Do you have a family history of osteoporosis?
- ☐ Are you Caucasian or Asian?
- ☐ Do you lead a sedentary lifestyle?
- ☐ Do you have chronically low dietary calcium intake?
- ☐ Are you fair, thin, and small boned or small framed?
- ☐ Have you had prolonged use of a cortisone medication?
- ☐ Do you smoke, drink coffee regularly, or eat red meat?
- ☐ Are you postmenopausal with a family history of osteoporosis?
- ☐ Have you had your ovaries removed before menopause?
- ☐ Did you have an early menopause before forty-five years of age?
- ☐ Have you used thyroid drugs for long periods of time?
- ☐ Have you lost height?

If you answered *yes* to any of these questions, you may do your own at-home test for osteoporosis to see if you are truly at risk: Using pH paper (found in drug stores), test your urine. A reading of pH 7 (acid) can mean calcium and bone loss. A reading above pH 7 indicates a low risk.

Don't forget to use nature's answer for these crippling diseases: Stop smoking and start exercising. Weight-bearing exercise is an excellent way to prevent bone loss and build bone. A walking program is very effective. (See chapter five.) Early morning sunbathing (before 10:00 a.m.) is also very effective and builds vitamin K in your body.

The most important factor in osteoporosis is the lack of progesterone, which causes a decrease in new bone growth. Adding progesterone will actively increase bone mass and density and can *reverse* osteoporosis. I recommend transdermal (topically applied to the skin) natural progesterone cream.

> ### 🌿 *Dr. Janet's Protocol for Osteoporosis*
>
> **NATURAL SUPPORT FOR OSTEOPOROSIS**
> - Natural progesterone cream
> - Eat a diet low in protein, focused on whole grains, leafy greens, and legumes. Avoid sodas and limit alcohol.
> - Vitamin D: 350–400 IU daily
> - Vitamin C: 2,000 mg a day in divided doses
> - Beta-carotene: 15 mg a day
> - Vitamin $B_6$: 50 mg daily
> - Zinc: 15–30 mg daily
> - Magnesium: 800 mg daily
> - Calcium: 1,500 mg daily

## NUTRITIONAL BALANCE AND AGING

As a woman ages, she has difficulty absorbing nutrients. In this section of the chapter we are going to look closely at some of the nutritional decisions we can make that will help us to balance our bodies physically during the aging process.

When digestive enzymes aren't working at their optimal level, deficiencies occur. This is especially true for B vitamins. To insure that you make up the difference, you should eat plenty of leafy greens and whole grains. Adding brewer's yeast and wheat germ to your meals will further strengthen you against vitamin B depletion. Make sure that you consume enough fiber daily, such as oats, whole grains, raw vegetables, and ground flaxseeds. This will help to reduce toxins in your digestive tract and prevent constipation. Boost healthful bacteria in your digestive tract by eating yogurt and other fermented foods such as sauerkraut and kefir. These sources of healthy bacteria help to fight infections.

Boost the antiaging powers of your next meal by adding fresh oregano. Shiow Wang, a scientist at the USDA's agricultural research service, tested the antioxidant action of twenty-one different fresh herbs. All varieties of oregano came out on top. Even more surprising was the fact that oregano's antioxidant activity exceeded that of vitamin E.[6]

Take vitamin C every day to help fight free-radical damage, strengthen your immune system, and reduce your cancer risk. Add foods that are good sources of vitamin C, such as citrus fruit, strawberries, tomatoes, asparagus, and green leafy vegetables. When you cook, add plenty of onion, garlic, or both to your dishes. Both have antioxidant and circulatory-boosting properties. Make sure to consume quality protein daily at every meal. This will help to give you energy and provide your body with slow, even-burning fuel throughout the day. Sources include fish, lean chicken and turkey, beans, and soy products. Lower your risk of heart disease, cancer, and arthritis by eating foods rich in vitamin E and selenium, such as nuts, seeds, and vegetable oils.

*Dr. Janet's Recommendation:*

Try flax, fiber, folic, and vitamin C if you have a bad Pap smear.[7]

As you age, dehydration becomes more of an issue. Make sure to stay well hydrated by drinking water every two hours whether you are thirsty or not. Staying well hydrated can help cut your risk of chronic constipation, fatigue, headaches, weight gain, kidney malfunction, and poor absorption of nutrients. Pure water will keep you hydrated and help all of your body's systems to work more efficiently. In addition, water will help proper elimination, remove toxins, lessen arthritic pain, and help to transport proteins, vitamins, minerals, and sugars for assimilation. Water helps the body work at its peak. Based on my research, dehydration is one of the main causes of hospital stays among elderly.[8]

To insure restful, recuperative sleep, eat complex carbohydrates, which can promote relaxation. Make sure to avoid caffeine, alcohol, or simple sugars in the evening as they will keep you awake or prevent a sound restorative sleep.

The following chart will give you a list of the best all-time longevity superfoods!

---

### ADD LIFE TO YOUR YEARS WITH GOOD NUTRITION!

- Avoid fried foods, red meat, too much caffeine, and highly spiced and processed foods.
- Eat fresh seafood at least twice weekly for thyroid health and balance.
- Have a green drink daily. I recommend Kyo-Green by Wakunaga.
- Nuts, seed, beans, fiber, and essential fatty acids are living nutrients.
- Fresh fruit is enzyme rich and full of vitamins, minerals, and fiber.
- Fresh vegetables are also enzyme rich and full of vitamins, minerals, and fiber.

---

Begin now to practice caloric reduction. As you age, your body requires fewer calories; it also burns calories at a lower rate. In addition, a low-calorie diet has been shown to protect your DNA from damage. This will thereby prevent organ and tissue degeneration. Try to get more "bang for your caloric buck" by eating only high-quality, densely nutritious foods at each meal. For example: eat fresh fruit and vegetables, organically grown if possible.

## ANTIAGING PROTOCOL

The following supplements are general recommendations to help you age, not just gracefully, but vibrantly.

- *CoQ$_{10}$:* Take 50–300 mg daily. It is an antioxidant and a cardiovascular health promoter. It also protects from periodontal disease or gum problems.
- *L-glutathione:* It is an antioxidant, amino acid that neutralizes radiation and inhibits free radicals.
- *Plant enzymes:* Take two capsules with each meal to inspire optimal digestion and utilization of nutrients.
- *Alpha lipoic acid:* Take 50 mg twice daily. It is one of the most important antioxidants in the body.

- *Cordyceps sinensis*: Take two to four capsules daily. It will help combat fatigue, boost immunity, and help fight the aging process. It is used often in Chinese medicine.
- *Reishi extract*: Take two to four capsules daily. It is another much used mushroom from the world of Chinese medicine to improve immunity and liver function.
- *Gingko biloba*: Take 60–120 mg twice daily. It improves circulation, improves hearing and vision, improves memory and brain activity, and has antioxidant properties.
- *Gota kola*: This supplement is used for brain and nervous system health.
- *Royal jelly*: An antiaging superfood, great for chronic fatigue and immune health, it is also a great source of pantothenic acid.
- *Lycopene*: An anticancer antioxidant, it reduces the risk of prostate and cervical cancer.
- *Germanium*: Germanium increases tissue oxygenation, thereby preventing disease.
- *Bilberry*: This supplement protects against macular degeneration.
- *Astragalus*: Used for adrenal health, this supplement helps to lower blood pressure and improves circulation.
- *Hawthorn berry*: It protects the heart from free-radical damage and helps the heart pump blood efficiently.
- *A green drink* daily, as directed, will help to detoxify your system and promote immunity, alkalinity, and healthy blood chemistry.
- *High-potency multivitamin/mineral formula*: This should be your foundation from which to add other supplements based upon your specific needs.
- *Aged garlic*: Take one to two capsules daily. Garlic, such as Kyolic, will boost the health of your cardiovascular and immune system.

- *Essential fatty acids*: They are even more essential as a woman ages. Take 2 tablespoons of flaxseed oil or 3 grams of fish oil or omega-3, omega-6, and omega-9 in a combination formula.
- Be sure to keep moving throughout your life. An exercise program will play a large role in the prevention of osteoporosis, obesity, heart disease, and arthritis.
- Reduce your stress levels, as nothing ages you faster.

By implementing these suggestions, you can stay one step ahead of degenerative disease and defy your age![9]

This chapter is probably one of the most important in this body of work. From the cradle to the grave, our hormones play a vitally important role in our health and well-being—so much so that hundreds of books have been written on the topic. Today's women are not sitting back and letting symptoms of hormonal imbalance or depletion destroy their lives, health, and peace of mind.

Women of today are fortunate to have access to much information and choices. Our mothers and grandmothers were not as fortunate, but for the most part, their hormonal issues were not as severe as the ones we face in this era. This is due in part to the amount of environmental and dietary xenoestrogens to which we are exposed on a daily basis. *Xenoestrogens* are substances that exert an estrogen-like effect on our systems, thereby contributing to hormonal imbalance due to estrogen dominance. It is this estrogen dominance that causes early puberty in young girls. When you add in lowered adrenal function (hypoadrenia), due to high-stress lifestyles, and poor diet, complete with high caffeine and sugar consumption, you have the makings of a nation of hormonally imbalanced women.

The good news is that whatever your stage of life—PMS, perimenopause, or menopause—there are answers from nature that can help you regain balance and reclaim your *edge*.

## PMS (PREMENSTRUAL SYNDROME)

It has been said that 90 percent of premenopausal women suffer some degree of PMS. The symptoms can last from two days to as long as two weeks and include headache, mood swings, acne, bloating, irritability, fatigue, tender breasts, anxiety, depression, low back pain, and more. PMS is believed to be caused by the hormonal shift in estrogen/progesterone levels during the menstrual cycle.

PMS results from inadequate levels of progesterone in the second half of the menstrual cycle. This creates an "estrogen dominant" situation. Estrogen dominance occurs more often in women these days because of xenoestrogens like environmental pollutants, pesticides, plastic-lined cans, stress, and beef, poultry, and milk laden with growth hormones.

*Dr. Janet's Recommendation:*

PMS? Try natural progesterone, borage seed oil, and grapeseed extract.[1]

Many women say that they experience most symptoms of PMS in the two-week period before menstruation, when the ratios are most elevated. In addition, low thyroid, low brain serotonin, poor liver function, and a diet that contains too much salt, caffeine, sugar, and red meat are all implicated in the development of PMS. It has been found that many sufferers have deficiencies in the B vitamins and in minerals. Emotional turmoil and stress can magnify the symptoms. Because of all of the factors that contribute to PMS, there is no one cause and no one treatment. Again, balance is key.

The following recommendations will provide your body with nutrition and the herbal support necessary for your body to come into balance and experience relief. These recommendations may take two to three months to take full effect. Once balance is achieved, please remember that you must be consistent and continue with the protocol in order to prevent a recurrence.

## PMS PROTOCOL

*Diet*

Your diet should be low fat with regular seafood consumption. Be sure to have plenty of cruciferous vegetables and dark leafy greens to reduce estrogen buildup associated with PMS (broccoli, cauliflower). Have brown rice often for B vitamins.

Buy organic meat, milk, milk products, and canned foods. Eliminate dairy during your PMS days.

Use whole grains, and keep your diet low in sugar and salt. Avoid caffeine and animal products.

Make sure to keep bowel function optimal. Add fiber to your diet. Take probiotics for friendly bowel flora. Drink plenty of water (at least six glasses daily). The chart below will give you protocols for several specific PMS symptoms.

### PREMENOPAUSE PROTOCOL

PMS sufferers have been grouped into four main categories by dividing the most common symptoms for which PMTS (premenstrual tension syndrome) patients seek medical advice and relief. I will give you protocols for each group.[2]

*PMT-A: anxiety, irritability, and nervous tension*
Recommendations:

- Magnesium: 400–600 mg daily
- Calcium: 800–1,200 mg daily
- B-complex vitamin: 1 daily
- Passionflower
- Valerian
- GABA
- Dr. Janet's Woman's Balance Formula transdermal progesterone cream

*PMT-C: increased premenstrual appetite, craving for sweets (mainly chocolate), refined sugar, resulting in fainting spells, fatigue, palpitation, and headache*
Recommendations:

- Dr. Janet's Woman's Balance Formula
- B-complex vitamin: 50–100 mg of each B vitamin
- Eat small meals throughout the day
- Chromium picolinate: 200 mcg daily; 400 mcg if over 150 pounds
- Calcium: 800–1,200 mg daily
- Magnesium: 400–800 mg daily

*PMT-D: depression, withdrawal, lethargic, suicidal tendencies, confusion, incoherence, difficulty verbalizing*
Recommendations:

- 5-HTP: as directed on the bottle
- B-complex vitamin: 100 mg of each of the B vitamins
- Magnesium: 400–800 mg daily
- Calcium: 800–1,200 mg daily
- Sleep Link, for insomnia
- Dr. Janet's Woman's Balance Formula transdermal progesterone cream

*PMT-H: premenstrual sensation of weight gain, abdominal bloating, tenderness, breast congestion, edema of face and extremities*
Recommendations:

- B-complex vitamin: one capsule twice daily
- Magnesium: 200–600 mg daily
- Vitamin E: 400–800 IU daily
- Evening primrose oil: 1,500 mg daily
- Calcium: 800–1,200 mg daily
- Potassium: 1–2 gm daily

*Exercise*

Use stretching exercises to help you with the symptoms of PMS. Keep your exercise schedule light. Breathe deeply, and spend twenty minutes in the sunshine each day if possible.

*Nutrition and supplementation*

To balance estrogen/progesterone ratio, use natural progesterone cream applied topically twice daily for two weeks before menstrual cycle begins.

Boost minerals by taking calcium (1,200 mg daily) and magnesium (400 mg) daily. A mood elevator you can use is 5-HTP. Take 25–50 mg at night.

For breast soreness/tenderness, eliminate caffeine and chocolate and use natural progesterone cream topically. You can also use evening primrose oil, 3,000 mg daily, and gingko biloba.

Treat yourself to a "premenstrual massage" each month. To relieve back pain, take quercetin (1,000 mg) or bromelain (1,500 mg), or use ginger packs on your lower back.

## PERIMENOPAUSE

Perimenopause occurs in women around the age of forty and continues until the early fifties when the menstrual period becomes a thing of the past, signaling the beginning of menopause. During this stage of life, many women experience a decrease or even cessation in their progesterone production because of irregular ovarian cycling and ovarian aging. At the same time, estrogen levels may be excessively or moderately high, causing a troubling continual state of imbalance. This condition is now recognized as "estrogen dominance." And therein lies most of the midlife woman's complaints.

Women may experience a plethora of symptoms, some for years on end. These may include fatigue, breast tenderness, foggy thinking, irritability, headaches, insomnia, decreased sex drive, anxiety, depression, allergy symptoms (including asthma), fat gain (especially around the middle), hair loss, mood swings, memory loss, water retention, bone

loss, endometrial cancer, breast cancer, slow metabolism, and many more. Hormonal imbalance has far-reaching effects on many tissues in the body, including the heart, brain, blood vessels, bones, uterus, and breasts.

The key to smooth perimenopause is bringing the levels of estrogen and progesterone back into balance as well as managing stress. Once this is accomplished, women feel wonderful again, complete with vitality, alertness, and optimism. They become more sociable and more nurturing to themselves and to others.

## Perimenopause Symptoms

Check any of the following symptoms that you are experiencing:

- ☐ Weight gain
- ☐ Sleep difficulties
- ☐ Lowered sex drive
- ☐ Anxiety/irritability
- ☐ Brain fog
- ☐ Breast cysts or breast tenderness
- ☐ Irregular menstrual cycles
- ☐ Fluid retention
- ☐ Mood swings
- ☐ Fibroid tumors
- ☐ Endometriosis
- ☐ Heavy, irregular menstrual bleeding

These symptoms indicate estrogen dominance, which is common during perimenopause.

In order to bring your estrogen and progesterone back into balance, I recommend using natural progesterone. It not only helps to restore balance, but it also helps to regulate thyroid activity. Natural progesterone is essential for the production of cortisone in the adrenal cortex, and it helps prevent breast cysts.

Natural progesterone has been found to be effective at combating perimenopausal anxiety and mood swings. In addition, it plays a very important part in the prevention and reversal of osteoporosis. Natural progesterone offers a woman all of these benefits without a high risk of side effects commonly found in conventional hormone replacement therapy (HRT). The recommended dosage for women in perimenopause is ¼ to ½ teaspoon applied to any clean area of the skin twice a day (morning and evening). I personally keep mine on my nightstand to insure that I never skip a dose. (Guidelines for perimenopausal progesterone use are based upon a 2-ounce container containing 960 mg total, or 40 mg per ½ teaspoon, 20 mg per ¼ teaspoon, or 10 mg per ⅛ teaspoon.)

### NATURAL PROGESTERONE USE

- Women who have had a complete hysterectomy (no ovaries, no uterus): 15–20 mg (¼ teaspoon) per day of progesterone for twenty-five days of the calendar month, with five to seven days without it.
- Women who have had a partial hysterectomy (no uterus, but still have ovaries): use ¼ to ½ teaspoon twice a day for three weeks out of the month.
- Women with endometriosis: use ¼ to ½ teaspoon of the cream from day 8 to 26 of your cycle.
- Premenopausal women who are menstruating but not ovulating: use ¼ to ½ teaspoon of a 2-ounce container per month. Begin using on day 10 to 12 of your cycle, and continue until your expected period.

Areas of application include chest, inner arms, neck, face, palms, and even soles of the feet if they are not calloused. Apply in the morning and again at bedtime.[3]

According to the late pioneer of progesterone therapy, John R. Lee, MD: "One of progesterone's most powerful and important roles in the body is to balance and oppose estrogen."[4]

The following list of estrogen and progesterone effects will further drive home the importance of natural progesterone use at midlife and beyond. I personally use natural progesterone each and every day, skipping the first week out of the month.

| Estrogen's Effects | Progesterone's Effects |
| --- | --- |
| Increases body fat | Helps use fat for energy |
| Increases salt and fluid retention | Acts as a natural diuretic |
| Increases risk of breast cancer | Helps prevent breast cancer |
| Decreases sex drive | Restores sex drive |
| Causes headaches and depression | Acts as a natural antidepressant |
| Impairs blood sugar control | Normalizes blood sugar levels |
| Increases risk of endometrial cancer | Prevents endometrial cancer |
| Reduces oxygen in all cells | Restores proper cell oxygen |

### Perimenopausal marvels

There are natural supplements that you can use to deal with any of the perimenopausal symptoms you are experiencing. Try the following marvels in your daily regime.

*Quercetin* is a potent antioxidant that reduces the inflammation of endometriosis. It also helps reduce estrogen and cholesterol levels, while boosting circulation and proper digestion. *Chaste tree berry* promotes progesterone production. *Bromelain* is a digestive

> *Dr. Janet's Recommendation:*
>
> If you do your best to maintain your physical, mental, and emotional balance through the mid cycle of your life, aging will be more graceful and less painful.[5]

enzyme that reduces pain and inflammation when taken between meals. You can also increase your intake of essential fatty acids by adding flaxseed to your diet. Essential fatty acids (EFAs) help to reduce pain due to bloating, breast tenderness, endometriosis, and menstrual cramping. They are also good for skin, hair, and the heart. Don't forget the benefits of vitamin C. Taking 600–2,000 mg daily can help you fight heart disease by preventing LDL oxidation. Take it in divided doses.

## MENOPAUSE

Do you have any of these symptoms?

- ☐ You're gaining weight.
- ☐ Your periods are irregular.
- ☐ You have been diagnosed with uterine fibroids.
- ☐ Your breasts are sore and lumpy.
- ☐ Your skin is drier, thinner, more wrinkled, and lacks that velvety texture.
- ☐ Your sex drive has decreased, and intercourse is painful.
- ☐ You're irritable, anxious, and maybe even depressed.
- ☐ You have frequent bladder or vaginal infections.
- ☐ Your joints and muscles ache.
- ☐ You forget small details.
- ☐ You've begun to experience "hot flashes" and "electric shocks" going through your body.
- ☐ You would do anything for a good night's sleep.

What's going on? Welcome to the transitional midlife stage known as the premenopausal/menopausal years. It is the time to fasten your seatbelt, because the roller-coaster ride is about to begin! It's time for you to understand the anatomy of a hot flash. Hot flashes are related to fluctuating estrogen levels. Hot flashes occur as a result of increased blood flow to the brain, skin, and organs, which causes a sudden sensation of warmth that may be followed by chills. At menopause, estrogen production drops by 75–90 percent, while progesterone production has virtually stopped. Androgens, the hormones that stimulate your sex drive, drop by 50 percent.

Dr. Eldred B. Taylor, medical director of the Department of Integrative Medicine at Dekalb Medical Center in Atlanta, has said: "Progesterone deficiency and estrogen excess are involved in most, if not all, the gynecological problems we diagnose and treat."[6] And it isn't only symptoms of hormonal imbalance that are bothering many midlife women. Many are also out of touch with their bodies and their feelings. Some have even lost touch socially as they try to balance work and family life. They do not nurture themselves and wind up tired, bewildered, anxious, and depressed.

It is unfortunate that many in the medical profession have tended to treat this phase of life as a disease state rather than a normal passage of life. In years past, women with these same symptoms were nurtured with herbs, reassurance, and time-tested wisdom from older women who had taken the journey before them. Today's lifestyles are even more hectic, and stress levels are relentlessly high, further driving hormone levels down.

Many in the medical profession have tried to deal with these negative symptoms that occur at midlife with prescription medications that elevate mood and alter the personality. Synthetic hormone replacement has been a standard of midlife care. Just recently, a landmark study was halted abruptly (The Woman's Health Initiative) when it was found early on that Prempro, a synthetic estrogen/progestin medication actually *increased* a women's risk of heart attack, stroke, and breast cancer.[7] The study was aborted due to the possibility of endangering the lives of the women in the study. Now, for the first time in several decades, both doctors and patients are rethinking midlife hormonal health. They both have heard, and research has now shown, that estrogen, when in excess, is a dangerous cancer promoter. It fuels endometrial growth (endometriosis), encourages fibroid growth, contributes to fibrocystic breasts, and causes weight gain, headaches, gallbladder problems, and heavier periods, just to name a few of the negatives.

*Urinary tract infections*

Menopause also puts women at increased risk of urinary tract infections due to the changing ratios of estrogen and progesterone. A reduced level of estrogen in a woman's system at midlife tends to enhance the adhesive qualities of the bladder's lining, thereby preventing proper bacterial removal upon urination. In addition, by the time a woman reaches midlife, the muscles of the pelvic floor are weakened as the result of previous pregnancies and deliveries. This can cause the bladder to sag, which in turn contributes to the growth of bacterial colonies. Aging itself, poor posture, spinal disorders, excessive abdominal fat, and chronic constipation are other contributing factors. Most often, however, *E. coli* bacterium traveling up the urethra is the culprit. If bladder infections are ignored due to hectic lifestyles and not addressed quickly, the kidneys can be infected as well, making it a much more serious condition that can lead to kidney failure. It is essential to begin attacking the infection at the first sign of discomfort. Bladder infection symptoms frequently include painful, frequent, and urgent urination with pain in the lower back and abdomen, chills, and fever as the body tries to fight the infection. The urine is often cloudy with a strong smell. Occasionally, traces of blood are seen.

You may purchase a UTI (urinary tract infection) home test kit to determine if you in fact do have a UTI. During the acute stage of UTI, take 2 tablespoons of apple cider vinegar and honey in water in the morning. Limit the use of a diaphragm, and urinate as soon as possible after intercourse. Drink a glass of warm water with ¼ teaspoon baking soda added, and place a ginger pack on the kidneys and a warm castor oil pack on the abdomen.

Cucurbita pepo (commonly known as pumpkinseed extract) offers support for healthy bladder and urinary tract function. In-vitro studies show that pumpkinseed extract modulates aromatase, which converts testosterone to estradiol in women. A decrease in the conversion helps to maintain healthy testosterone levels in women, thus benefiting pelvic muscles and bladder function. Pumpkinseed extract has also been found to help postmenopausal women maintain healthy daytime and nighttime urination.

You will also support the function of your urinary tract by exercising and drinking eight glasses of water daily. You will know if you have strengthened your urinary tract when bladder infections and irritation cease, the flow of urine is increased, and you feel lighter and not so "bogged down." Fruits such as watermelon, celery, and blueberries will help to keep your system alkalinized. Kegel exercises will help urinary incontinence.

## THE ESTROGEN CROSSROAD

Midlife women today are at a crossroad. Do they take estrogen and risk hormone-related cancer later on, or do they suffer in silence as their bodies ache and rapidly age? Do they live in a hormone-deficient state and subject themselves to the possibility of acquiring the degenerative diseases that attack a body lacking proper balance? The good news is that you don't have to suffer and fall victim to accelerated aging and degenerative health conditions.

Let's talk about why a natural transition is best. It is common knowledge that the risks associated with conventional HRT have filled medical journals for more than twenty years. In 1975, the *New England Journal of Medicine* said that estrogen significantly increased the risk of cancer of the uterine lining.[8] In 1997, *Lancet* stated that conventional HRT increased the risk of breast cancer with each year of use.[9] And in 2000, the *Journal of the American Medical Association* wrote that women who took combined treatment (estrogen/progesterone) for five years had a 40 percent greater chance of developing breast cancer than women taking estrogen alone or no hormones.[10]

The good news is that you do not have to suffer with the symptoms of accelerated aging and degenerative health conditions that often result from conventional HRT therapy. There are many natural supplements that can be just as effective—and more—for dealing with the onset of menopause. In the following chart, I want to give you a protocol for dealing with menopause naturally.

## Dealing With Menopause Naturally

### BLACK COHOSH
*Dosage*: 80–160 mg daily
Black cohosh alleviates anxiety, hot flashes, night sweats, vaginal dryness and atrophy, depression, heart palpitations, headaches, and sleep disturbances. (Note: Do not take black cohosh if you are taking a prescription for conventional HRT.)[11]

### FLAXSEED
*Dosage*: oil, capsules as directed, or flaxseeds 2 Tbsp. daily
Flaxseed helps keep the skin supple and the vaginal tissues to become healthy. It also helps the body produce prostaglandins (inflammation fighters).

### VITAMIN E
*Dosage*: 400–1,600 IU daily
Vitamin E reduces the risk of heart attack and stroke. It is a skin nutrient and mood balancer, and it relieves hot flashes.

### PROGESTERONE CREAM
*Dosage*: ¼ to ½ teaspoon applied to any clean area of the skin twice a day (morning and evening)
Natural progesterone can balance the ratio of estrogen and progesterone, thereby alleviating all of the symptoms of estrogen dominance. In addition, it helps to build bone and helps to relieve anxiety and protects against breast cancer.[12]

### DONG QUAI (*ANGELICA SINENIS*)
*Dosage*: 250–500 mg daily
Dong quai has phytoestrogen activity and has been called female ginseng because of its ability to enhance energy and a sense of well-being.

### FIBER
*Dosage*: Add high-fiber foods to your daily diet or take a fiber supplement. Fiber is crucial because women who

are constipated have four times the risk of breast cancer. To determine the ideal amount of fiber you need for optimal health, visit http://www.healthcalculators .org/calculators/fiber.asp, provided as a public service by the University of Maryland Medical System.

### GAMMA ORYZANOL
*Dosage*: 300 mg daily derived from rice bran oil
Gamma oryzanol diminishes hot flashes, headaches, sleeplessness, and mood swings.

## THE CASE FOR BIOIDENTICAL
## HORMONE REPLACEMENT THERAPY

I believe that in our younger days, our bodies made ample hormones to keep us young, healthy, and vibrant. As the years pass, our bodies do not produce hormones in the balanced amounts that keep us feeling energized. What do we do? The answer is simple. We can turn to the plant kingdom, where natural hormones abound. Soybeans, black cohosh, Mexican wild yam, and licorice can be of benefit to a perimenopausal/menopausal woman. But for many women, stressful lifestyles have made it necessary to move up to bioidentical hormones that are derived from these plants and then synthesized in a lab to be molecularly similar to the hormones our bodies make.

*Do you need bioidentical hormone replacement?*

First, get your hormone levels tested. I recommend the ZRT Saliva Test Kit developed by Dr. David Zava and Dr. John Lee. Test your hormone levels before you begin any natural hormone replacement program; test them again after six months to see the progress made. This test should check progesterone, estradiol, estrone, estriol, testosterone, androstenedione, DHEA-S, and cortisol. Most women only test estradiol and progesterone levels. I believe you should check all these levels; then a hormone replacement program can be tailored especially for you based upon your results. Once you know where your levels are, you can choose to take bioidentical hormones, which are identical to the hormones that your body naturally produces.

*Just what are bioidentical hormones?*

Unlike synthetic hormones, which the drug companies purposely make different in order to patent the drugs (such as Prempro, Provera, and Premarin), bioidenticals have the same molecular structure as the hormones (progesterone, estrogen, DHEA, etc.) that your own body creates, hence the name *bioidentical hormones.*

Bioidentical hormones are much safer for your body because they are easier for your body to metabolize without many of the side effects that synthetic hormones create. They have been shown to increase your energy, reduce facial hair, improve your sense of well-being, improve memory, aid weight loss, increase libido, and boost energy. Conversely, synthetic hormones have side effects that include lack of sex drive, poor sleep, increased cancer risk, and weight gain. In addition to bioidentical hormone replacement, make sure to clean up your diet, eat well and often, get plenty of rest, drink plenty of water (half your body weight in ounces daily), and take a calcium supplement and a good daily multivitamin. Make sure to attend to the health of your adrenal glands, because they play an important role in your hormone balance!

When it comes to testing hormones, which test is better: blood test or saliva test? A saliva test is more preferable, more affordable, and more accurate than a blood test. The advantage of a saliva test is that it allows for the hormone levels to be tested accurately because saliva

---

*Dr. Janet's Recommendation:*

The good news is that you can test your hormones in the privacy of your own home.

You may order your own Saliva Hormone Test Kit from :
*ZRT Laboratory*
*Info@zrtlab.com*
*Phone: 503-466-2445*
*Hormone Hotline: 503-466-9166 (24 hour taped audio library)*

Please note that some states require that your physician order these tests.

contains only the unbound biologically active hormones. A blood test is unable to test the biologically active hormones.

Menopause can vary widely between each individual. Many factors influence the timing of menopause, including trauma, surgery, and low body weight, which brings on early menopause due to decreased hormone output by the ovaries. Anorexia can cause the ovaries to shut down completely. Being overweight can delay menopause because extra fat increases estradiol.

Physically active and well-nourished women experience late menopause while smokers experience earlier menopause. Adrenal exhaustion from too much stress and poor diet can cause early menopause. Here are some of the simple things that you can do to make this complex season of your life more balanced.

**SIMPLIFYING MENOPAUSE**

Follow these dietary guidelines while experiencing the symptoms of menopause:

- Add soy foods to your diet.
- Limit sugar, caffeine, pies, cakes, and pastries.
- Limit red meat.
- Eat fresh vegetables, fruits, and nuts.
- Eat small meals throughout the day instead of three large ones.
- Limit dairy products

There are also many natural herbal remedies that will alleviate your menopause symptoms and help you find balance in this season. I suggest that you try them one by one, and determine for yourself the ones that really give you comfort.

- Evening primrose oil: 1,300 mg three times daily
- Black currant seed oil
- Dong quai, which is high in phytoestrogens
- Red raspberry

- Licorice, which is important for your adrenal health
- Dr. Janet's Woman's Balance Formula (progesterone cream)
- Black cohosh
- Bioflavonoids, which are high in phytoestrogens
- Plant enzymes, taken with meals
- Vitamin C
- Vitamin E, a hormone normalizer
- B-complex vitamin
- Raw female glandular
- Adrenal glandular
- 5-HTP, for insomnia and anxiety at night

It will be important for you to make some important lifestyle changes also. Be sure to do the following on a daily basis:

- Exercise (I recommend Pilates exercise and weight-bearing exercises.)
- Laughter
- Massage therapy
- Deep breathing

Menopause does not signal the end of your vitality, attractiveness, and purpose in life. It is a time of reevaluation and a time to focus on the rest of your life. It is an opportunity to accomplish the desires of your heart. It is a time of wisdom and a time for sharing that wisdom and talents that are uniquely yours. Many women experience "post-menopausal zest" for life. It is a wonderful time of service, self-discovery, and spiritual maturity.

### Dr. Janet's Recommended Reading

- Christiane Northrup, MD, *The Wisdom of Menopause* (New York: Bantam Books, 2001)

- John R. Lee, MD, with Virginia Hopkins, *What Your Doctor May Not Tell You About Menopause* (New York: Warner Books, 1999)

- Judith Reichman, MD, *Relax, This Won't Hurt* (New York, William Morrow and Co., 2000)

According to a research study conducted in 1994, more than a quarter million working women surveyed said that their primary concern was the difficulty they had balancing work and family. Half of those women stated that "too much stress" was a serious problem for them.[1] The study showed that women were more likely than men to report stress, and they reacted to a wider range of stressors. These same women were studied again in 2000 and 2001, and it was discovered that those who suffered high stress in 1994 and 1995 had higher odds of developing a number of chronic conditions by 2000 or 2001.[2]

When stress is ignored, it can escalate to *distress*. A woman who is distressed is headed for burnout and total exhaustion. Stress is your body's signal that your life needs attention. Do not ignore it! Take it as a sign telling you that you need to acknowledge your limitations, make a decision, meet a need, or take time out to rest.

When it comes to stress, it has been said, "If you do not take the time to be well, you will definitely take the time to be sick." Stress, when not addressed, makes women vulnerable to emotional and physical illness, such as anxiety, illness, heart attacks, and depression.

To balance your life you must develop a balanced lifestyle that includes friends, family, work, play, love, time for self, and time for spiritual growth. A well-rounded life—one balanced physically, emotionally, and spiritually—leads to a greater sense of well-being. Every woman is different. What

stresses your best friend Jane may not stress you. It is how you perceive things. A *stressor* is any demand good or bad that is made upon your body or mind. Stressors can be caused by external pressures, such as a bad work environment, or internal pressures, such as feeling that you must compete or that you are not good enough or that caring for your needs is selfish.

To start the healing process, you must identify the causes of your stress and the effects it has on your body, mind, and spirit. If there are situations in your life that are stressing you that are unchangeable, then you must learn to stop expending so much of your precious emotional energy on the situations and begin to focus on areas for which you can find solutions.

*Dr. Janet's Recommendation:*

You must not neglect yourself as you try to meet everyone else's needs, both at home and at work.

The following symptoms are commonly associated with stress overload.

## BACKGROUND CHECK

Check each symptom you are experiencing:

- ☐ Headaches
- ☐ Muscle tension
- ☐ Anger
- ☐ Irritability
- ☐ Anxiety
- ☐ Sleeplessness
- ☐ Indigestion
- ☐ Burnout
- ☐ High blood pressure
- ☐ Lack of appetite
- ☐ Inability to concentrate
- ☐ Depression

☐    Decreased sexual interest

If you can relate to any of these symptoms, you must take steps now to prevent emotional and physical illness in the future.

## STRESS AND YOU

As we begin this chapter, take this self-assessment survey, developed by the Midwest Center for Stress and Anxiety, to find out just how much emotional stress and pain are contributing to your current state of health and imbalance. There are common backgrounds in people who suffer from anxiety, chronic illness, and emotional fatigue.

### BACKGROUND CHECK

Check the ones that apply to you:

*Childhood*

☐    Unstable upbringing/divorce of parent

☐    Lack of approval and praise

☐    Feeling that you must prove yourself as a child

☐    Strict religious upbringing/guilt and fear

☐    Siblings parenting other siblings

☐    Nervous disorders in family

☐    Separation or loss of a family member

☐    Strict parents with high expectations

☐    Family history of alcoholism

☐    Low self-esteem

☐    Feelings not easily shown or displayed

There are several personality traits that are adopted because of our childhood experiences. The following traits are commonly found in people who suffer from anxiety, stress-related disorders, and emotional pain.

Check the ones that you can identify with:

- ☐ Tendency to overreact
- ☐ Perfectionist
- ☐ Inner nervousness
- ☐ Emotionally sensitive
- ☐ Guilt ridden
- ☐ Extremely analytical
- ☐ Overly concerned about others' opinions of you
- ☐ Obsessive thinker
- ☐ Worry about health problems
- ☐ High expectations
- ☐ Inability to make decisions

## THE BODY-MIND CONNECTION

When your emotional pain becomes full-fledged anxiety, you may experience any of the following symptoms.

- Fatigue
- Muscle tension
- Strange aches and pains
- Migraine headaches
- Depression
- Dizziness
- Hot and cold flashes
- Nausea
- Racing heart
- Disorientation
- Panic attacks
- Scary thoughts
- Sweats

If you are experiencing these symptoms, you must begin to balance your emotional health and reduce your emotional stress as you begin to balance your physical symptoms of stress. Don't become discouraged. Your Creator has created you with the ability to live in balance—body, mind, and spirit. Remember what the Bible has promised us:

> No test or temptation [or stress] that comes your way is beyond the course of what others have had to face. All you need to remember is that God will never let you down; he'll never let you be pushed past your limit; he'll always be there to help you come through it.
> —1 CORINTHIANS 10:13, THE MESSAGE

## FOUR LEVELS OF STRESS

Now, let's look at the four levels of stress. This will help you to determine what level your stress has brought you to.

### FOUR LEVELS OF STRESS

#### LEVEL I

- Losing interest in enjoyable activities
- Sagging of the corners of the eyes
- Creasing of the forehead
- Becoming short tempered
- Bored, nervous

#### LEVEL II

All of level I, plus:

- Tiredness, anger, insomnia, paranoia, sadness

#### LEVEL III

All of levels I and II, plus:

- Chronic head and neck aches
- High blood pressure
- Upset stomach
- Looking older

**LEVEL IV**

All of levels I, II, and III, plus:

- ⮞ Skin disorders
- ⮞ Kidney malfunction
- ⮞ Frequent infections
- ⮞ Asthma
- ⮞ Heart disease
- ⮞ Mental or emotional breakdown

## RECOVERY FROM STRESS

A certain amount of stress is normal—and necessary—in everyone's life. Without the stress of the alarm clock every morning, many of us would fail to get up in time to meet the daily responsibilities. Some women even respond better to some stress than if no stress is present in their lives. But nearly every woman today has more stressors in her life than is healthy. You must take action and determine now to bring more balance into your life by getting rid of some of the stress that is robbing you of good health now and creating an atmosphere for chronic health conditions in the future.

Start today by considering your life and the stress you are facing. Answer the following questions:

1. What is really important in my life?

_____

_____

_____

2. What do I want to achieve for myself?

_____

_____

_____

3. For my family?

_____

_____

4.  Who are the important people in my life?

    _____

    _____

    _____

5.  How will I give priority to the things that are most important?

    _____

    _____

    _____

Once you have taken inventory of your life, you can begin to develop a plan of attack for dealing with—and getting rid of—some of the stress in your life. Consider the following suggestions for your plan of attack.

1.  Say *no* to added demands on your personal time.
2.  Be more flexible, and forget about being *perfect!* Just do your best.
3.  Make fun and relaxation a part of your daily and long-term plans.
4.  Value yourself and what you do.
5.  Get outside help for household responsibilities if needed.
6.  Focus on your accomplishments, and do not dwell on your shortcomings.
7.  Take care of *you;* invest in your health.
8.  Exercise to release anger.
9.  Don't take life too seriously; laugh often.
10. Establish networks of support, friendship, and cooperation in your community.
11. Delegate responsibilities to others.
12. Take time to organize your home and workplace, and keep track of events, due dates, and commitments.[3]

In addition to these suggestions, consider also the following recovery points for you to remember.

- Expecting perfection leads to stress.
- You must respond positively to life events. You do have a choice.
- Stressors are rooted in your daily habits and the ways that you "talk to yourself" about what has happened.
- Unmanaged stress can cause disease.
- Stress can result from major life events, such as disease, or from the accumulation of "daily hassles."
- Stress has a cumulative effect.

## HOW TO BEAT STRESS

It is possible to beat stress before it beats you! By following the tips and guidelines you have learned in this chapter—and in the preceding chapters—you can begin to bring physical, emotional, and spiritual balance into your life. Balance is the key to beating stress. As you prepare to make the guidelines you are learning from this book a part of your daily life, remember too to incorporate the following tips for beating stress.

- *Simplify your life.* Take inventory of how you spend your time, money, and energy; determine whether you really want or need everything you currently invest in. Can anything go without sacrificing personal or family happiness? Cut unnecessary stressful activities out of your life. Say *no* the next time you are asked to take on a new responsibility if you are already overextended from doing too much.
- *Get enough sleep.* Most women don't. If you have trouble falling asleep, an evening routine can help you. Don't drink caffeine or exercise late in the day, and keep a regular bedtime, adjusting it no more than an hour on weekends.
- *Eat well.* Besides choosing healthy foods, make mealtimes a pleasant social encounter. Celebrate family time by making menu planning, table setting, and cooking together family activities.

- *Exercise.* It triggers chemical reactions in our bodies, it enhances our moods, it makes us more fit to handle physical challenges, and it doesn't have to be structured. Look for opportunities to move—park farther from your destination for a longer walk, take the stairs instead of the elevator, or toss a ball with your family in the backyard.

- *Have fun.* Keep good balances of work and play, and of solitary and group activities. Sometimes we need time alone to gather our thoughts; sometimes we need people around to hug, listen to, or share ideas with us.

- *Maintain a support system.* Make sure your schedule accommodates time with loved ones. Think of recreational activities you can do with friends or family that don't cost much. If you struggle with a disease or a circumstance such as single parenthood, join a support group.

- *Meditate, pray.* Find ways to focus energy on a meaning and purpose beyond your everyday life.

- *Keep your sense of humor.* Laughter releases tension. Look for what's funny in everyday life. Find classic comedies on television or in the library's video section.

- *Be assertive.* Don't bottle up negative emotions and experiences. When you have a difficult message to deliver, describe the situation, express your feelings, specify your wants, and say it directly to the person involved. Write it down first or practice verbally, if that will help.

- *Be creative.* Indulge in enjoyable hobbies, whether they be painting, gardening, dancing, writing in a journal, or singing in a church choir or by yourself.

- *Give of yourself.* Finding a way to help someone in need is the best way to remind ourselves to be grateful for what we might take for granted.

- *Pamper yourself.* It doesn't cost much to relax with a long bubble bath, a foot bath while reading the mail, or a series of family back rubs.[4]

*Use your MANTLE for stress relief.*

When faced with stress and tension in my own life, I have found that my muscles tighten all over my body, and I generally feel miserable. Through research I discovered that both physical and emotional stress get stored in your muscles, making you even more tense. I want to share with you a wonderful technique that will work for you time and time again when you are faced with a body that is tight with stressed muscles. I call it the *MANTLE technique*. I continue to use it even as I am writing this book to relieve the tightness in my neck and shoulders. What is it? It is very simple. Simply tense each part of your body, one section at a time, and hold for the count of ten. You will find that you need your *mantle* every day:

**M**  muscles
**A**  always
**N**  need
**T**  tension
**L**  loosening
**E**  every day

Begin with your eyes…tense and hold for ten seconds, then release. Take a deep cleansing breath, filling your diaphragm with air and exhaling slowly through your mouth. Next, tighten all of the muscles of your face and mouth; make a face and hold it for ten seconds. Take another deep-cleansing breath. Continue this tensing and releasing exercise on down to the other parts of your body, including your neck, shoulders, arms, hands, fingers, stomach, lower abdomen, upper thighs, calves, feet, and toes. After each area has been relaxed, use this time for prayer and reflection.

### Dr. Janet's Protocol for Stress

*Natural "stress-busters"*

- *Siberian ginseng* is a root that belongs to the ginseng family of adaptogenic herbs. Adaptogens help build our resistance to stress. Siberian ginseng helps the body adapt to stress and lessens fatigue, often the underlying factors in the anxiety picture. It improves oxygen and blood sugar metabolism as well as immune function. Take daily for two to three months; then take a two-week break before resuming.

Since Siberian ginseng is a stimulant, do not take it before bed or if you have high blood pressure. It is not for severe anxiety. See your doctor if your symptoms are severe. One last tip: do not confuse Siberian ginseng with Panax ginseng, because Panax ginseng can increase your levels of cortisol, the body's stress hormone.

- *Valerian* is widely used in Europe as a sedative. It is also used in Chinese medicine to treat nervous conditions and insomnia. Its effect is said to be similar to benzodiazepine tranquilizers, but without side effects. Valerian works like benzodiazepines by enhancing the activity of GABA, the naturally tranquilizing neurotransmitter.

  Take 300–900 mg of valerian extract (standardized to 0.8 percent valeric acid) one hour before bedtime for insomnia; 50–100 mg taken two to three times a day may help relieve performance anxiety and stress. Do not take valerian with alcohol. Side effects are rare but may include headache and stimulant effects in some people. The effects of valerian use are cumulative, so you have to take it for two to three weeks before evaluating your results.

- *Passionflower* is a climbing plant, native to North America. Combined with valerian, passionflower is a popular herbal remedy throughout much of Europe for insomnia, anxiety, and irritability.

- *St. John's wort* has been used to treat anxiety and depression in Europe for twenty-four hundred years. Pretty impressive, wouldn't you say? St. John's wort is a natural substance that enhances the activity of GABA. In addition, it enhances the activity of three important neurotransmitters: serotonin, norepinephrine, and dopamine.

The standardized dose is 300-mg extract (standardized to 0.3 percent hypericin) three times per day. St. John's wort must be taken for six weeks before evaluating your results, because the effect is cumulative and not immediate. Do not take St. John's wort if you are currently taking prescription antidepressants, especially MAO inhibitors (such as Nardil or Parnate). If you stop taking a prescription antidepressant, wait at least four weeks before taking St. John's wort to make sure that no overlapping occurs. Side effects are very rare but include dizziness and gastrointestinal irritation.

*Kava*, the root of piper methysticum and a member of the pepper tree, is native to the South Pacific area. Kava has a natural tranquilizing effect on the brain by producing a soothing effect in the amygdala, the *alarm center* of the brain. The recommended dosage is 70–85 mg (70 percent kavalactones), taken in the evening. You may increase the dose to as much as 100 mg three times daily, if necessary.

Do not mix kava with alcohol, pharmaceutical antidepressants, benzodiazepine, tranquilizers, or sleeping pills. If you have Parkinson's disease, you should not take kava because it may worsen muscular weakness. Extremely high doses of kava (ten times the normal dose) can cause vision, breathing, and muscle problems. Yellowing and scaly skin has also occurred at high doses. Kava, if used properly, can bring blessed relief.[5]

5-HTP is derived from the seed of the Griffonia tree and is related to the amino acid tryptophan. It is used to alleviate anxiety, insomnia, depression, and other related conditions linked with low levels of serotonin. 5-HTP is a raw material the body uses to manufacture serotonin, the neurotransmitter linked with mood. By raising serotonin levels in the body, anxiety and depression can be relieved. Informal studies suggest that 5-HTP is effective for mild, moderate anxiety and full-blown anxiety disorders. The most effective study dose range was 75–100 mg per day. You should start with 25 mg per day at the time of the day when you feel most anxious.[6]

### ADRENAL EXHAUSTION—WIRED...BUT TIRED!

When Jane turned forty, she noticed that she had a difficult time getting up in the morning. She experienced continuing fatigue that was not relieved by sleep. She craved salty foods. She was lethargic, and everything seemed like a chore. It took increased effort for her to accomplish everyday tasks. In addition, she found that she had a decreased ability to handle stress. Romantic interludes with her husband were not appealing at all, because she barely had enough energy to keep going each day. The respiratory infection she caught in August was still hanging on in late September, and she found herself getting lightheaded when she stood up quickly. It was hard for her to concentrate, and her memory was poor. This made her mildly depressed. Something that Jane thought odd was the fact that she felt better after dinner and during late evening hours when her energy seemed to return. Jane was suffering from the classic symptoms of low adrenal function.

"Your biography becomes your biology."

Today, many women suffer from an often misunderstood, unrecognized, and underdiagnosed condition that often smolders just below the surface. It is known as *hypoadrenia*, or adrenal exhaustion. Weighing less than a cherry and no larger than a prune, each of your two adrenal glands sit perched atop your kidney. From this vantage point, they greatly affect the functioning of every single tissue, gland, and organ in your body. In addition, they also have a profound effect on the way you think and feel. At midlife, your energy, endurance, and your very life depend heavily on proper adrenal function. It is at midlife that a majority of Americans may suffer from some degree of adrenal meltdown.[7] There seems to be an epidemic of it due to excessive physical, emotional, and environmental stress.

Women experiencing low adrenal function often experience the following symptoms: low blood pressure, fatigue, lethargy, changes in sex drive (usually low or nonexistent), electrolyte and fluid imbalance, and changes in fat metabolism and in the heart and cardiovascular system. In addition, the body shape can change to more of an "apple" due to excess fat distribution in the midsection. People with low adrenal function live with a feeling of general unwellness. Coffee, teas, colas, chocolate, and other stimulants are often depended upon to keep their energy levels up long enough to make it through the day. These substances only tax the adrenals more, which in turn creates a vicious cycle or merry-go-round, if you will, that is hard to break out of.

Low blood sugar is also a part of the hypoadrenic picture, as well as allergies, asthma, low immunity, and arthritic pain. A woman's mental health is also affected by poor adrenal health. Symptoms include anxiety, depression, fearfulness, difficulty concentrating, confusion, and frustration. If the condition is ignored, hypoadrenia can lay the foundation for more serious health conditions such as fibromyalgia, asthma, autoimmune disorders, diabetes, and respiratory infections.

*Dr. Janet's Recommendation:*

Stress hits you in your hypothalamus, causing an imbalance in your ratio of estrogen and progesterone; it also triggers excessive output of adrenal hormones. Try vitamin C, fiber, B vitamins, indole-3-carbinol, and exercise to relieve and release stress.[8]

Hypoadrenia often occurs at midlife. Why is midlife the most common time for hypoadrenia to surface? The answer is simple…stress. Midlife, unlike any other period, often deals us many stressful life-changing events. We have experienced raising a family and all of the stress (good and bad) that goes along with it. We have built careers, and we strove to have happy marriages and families. We may have had an operation or two, and we may have lost a job, a dear friend, a parent, or even the beloved family pet. We may have had a car accident, have been bankrupt, divorced, had in-law problems, and worked too much and played too little, but most of all, we may not have taken the time to develop a close personal relationship with God.

Adrenal fatigue is usually triggered or caused by stress, whether it be from a low-grade infection, physical stress, emotional turmoil, or psychological distress. Your adrenal glands are affected by every kind of stress. The adrenals are much like batteries that are drained each time a stressor affects our life. If these batteries are not recharged by resting enough, eating a proper diet, and supplementing the body with adrenal-specific nutrients...if you have not forgiven enough in your personal life, not exercised enough...if you continue to consume stimulants (caffeine, colas, teas, etc.), an adrenal meltdown is possible.

It is harder to rebuild your system after a meltdown occurs. Prevention is far and away the best route to take. Too many traumatic events and relentless stress affect your adrenal glands' ability to rebound and recover. Over time, adrenal exhaustion may become the only state that you know. Women who suffer from this condition will often say, "I feel like I am just existing," or "I don't know where I went." There are certain personality traits common to persons with low adrenal function.

### Low Adrenal Function Common Personality Traits

Do these traits describe you?

- Perfectionist
- Lack of sleep
- Being driven
- Use of stimulants
- "A-type" personality
- Lack of leisure time and activities
- Keeping late hours
- Staying in no-win situations (this creates stress and frustration)

It is during midlife, when women are struggling just to keep up with daily demands, that the adrenals need to be strengthened and fortified.

This is especially true for the premenopausal/menopausal women. At midlife, the adrenals are designed to do *double duty* and pick up the slack for the ovaries as they begin to shut down their production of sex hormones. If the adrenals are taxed and worn out, they cannot help smooth out the transition into menopause.

This is when many A-type women experience an almost unbearable menopause, complete with severe anxiety, monster hot flashes, extreme fatigue, and more. These women are often prescribed Paxil, Xanax, and the like just to get them through these transitional years while at the same time sparing their families from dealing with Mom and her emotional imbalance. The good news is that you can recover from this condition that robs many women of vibrant health and joy.

If you want to see just how well your adrenal glands are performing, try this self-test. First, lie down and rest for five minutes. Then, take your blood pressure. Stand up immediately and take your blood pressure reading once more. If your blood pressure is lower after you stand up, you probably have reduced adrenal gland function, which means your batteries need a charge. The lower the blood pressure reading is from your resting blood pressure, the more severe the low adrenal function. The systolic number (or the number on top of the blood pressure reading) normally is about ten points higher when you are standing than when you lie down. A difference of more than ten points should be addressed immediately as it is of extreme importance in the journey back to health.

I recommend that you feed your worn-out adrenals the following supplements to bring them back to full power.

*Pantothenic acid*, a B vitamin known as an antistress vitamin, plays a role in the production of adrenal hormones. It is very helpful in alleviating anxiety and depression by fortifying the adrenal glands. In addition, pantothenic acid is needed to produce our own natural pain relievers, which include cortisol. This is very important because pain often goes hand in hand with emotional depletion.

*B-complex vitamins,* consisting of the full spectrum of B vitamins, help to maintain a healthy nervous system. B-complex vitamins come in two standard doses—50 mg and 100 mg. I recommend 50 mg as the daily dosage for most people, because the majority of people are taking a multivitamin that has B vitamins in it.

*Vitamin C* is required for tissue growth and repair, and for healthy gums and adrenal gland function. Vitamin C also protects us against infection and strengthens our immunity. In this context I will just mention the effect that vitamin C has on the adrenals.[9]

*Royal jelly* (2 teaspoonfuls daily) is known to be a blessing for the body against asthma, liver disease, skin disorders, and immune suppression. This is because it is rich in vitamins, minerals, enzymes, and hormones. In addition, it possesses antibiotic and antibacterial properties. It is interesting to note that it naturally contains a high concentration of pantothenic acid.

*Astragalus* (taken as directed on the bottle) is an herb that aids adrenal gland function. It also combats fatigue and protects the immune system. This herb played a large part in fortifying and strengthening my body when I battled the Epstein-Barr virus. It truly is a powerful herb in terms of immune boosting.

*L-tyrosine* is an amino acid that helps to build the body's natural supply of adrenaline and thyroid hormones. It converts to L-dopa, which makes it a safe therapy for depression. If you are on antidepressants or have cancer, you should avoid tyrosine. L-tyrosine supports the production of catecholamine neurotransmitters, enhancing mood and cognitive function especially in situations involving stress or when dopamine, epinephrine, or norepinephrine levels require additional support.[10]

*Adrenal complex glandular* is a dietary supplement that contains bovine adrenal tissue concentrate, which helps to support and strengthen the adrenal glands.[11]

### WARNING SIGNS OF ADRENAL EXHAUSTION

*Causes*: unrelenting stress, A-type personality, and long-term use of cortico-steroid drugs for asthma, arthritis, and allergies; too much sugar and caffeine in the diet; deficiency of vitamins

B and C. Adrenal exhaustion is also common during the peri-menopausal and menopausal stage of life.

*Warning signs*

- Severe reactions to odors or certain foods
- Recurring yeast infections
- Heart palpitations and panic attacks
- Dry skin and peeling nails
- Clammy hands and soles of feet
- Low energy and poor memory
- Chronic low back pain
- Cravings for salt and sugar

If you suspect that you may be suffering from adrenal exhaustion, you can jump-start your batteries by following this protocol for adrenal restoration.

## Adrenal Restoration

- Rest, rest, rest!
- Vitamin C, 3,000–4,000 mg daily in divided doses
- Pantothenic acid, 100 mg three times daily
- Adrenal glandular supplement as directed on bottle
- Amino acid L-tyrosine, 500 mg daily
- Dietary: brown rice, almonds, garlic, salmon, flounder, lentils, sunflower seeds, bran, brewer's yeast, and avocado.
- Royal jelly, 2 tsp. daily

As part of your balancing act, you must use a three-part plan of attack. First, exercise is a huge stress alleviator, which helps to bring down high levels of cortisol. It increases endorphins and serotonin, which will inhibit the stress response. Exercise just thirty minutes a day, five times a week, and add strength training two times a week. Be sure to take breaks throughout your day to diffuse your stress. Just taking the dog for a walk will work wonders! Breathe deeply, and reflect on all your blessings.

Nutrition is the next area you must address. Eliminate refined sugars and carbohydrates, and eat four to five servings of fruit and vegetables and three servings of whole grains daily. This will keep you energized and less apt to *stress eat.*

Finally, the mental aspect of stress management is to realize that stress is not stress unless you perceive it as stress. It is how you react and act that will determine if it will be detrimental to your health. When you realize that stress can drive up blood pressure, increase your risk for stroke, raise cortisol levels, change your body composition, increase your risk for degenerative disease, and rob you of energy and zest for life, you must become proactive by taking the steps I outlined for you in this chapter.

Life is meant to be lived with vibrancy, productivity, and creative expression. Stress is a great robber of health and of living life to the fullest.

Achieving balance in your life cannot be fully realized without understanding the importance of a woman's relationships—including your intimate relationships, your interactions and relationships in community with others, and your relationship with your Creator. The importance of purpose, the impact of being connected or belonging to something larger that yourself, and the peace and satisfaction that come from putting service before self have huge implications toward helping you to live in balance—physically, emotionally, and spiritually.

## A WOMAN AND INTIMACY

From the very moment of conception we experience intimacy with our mother that crystallizes when we are held in her arms on the day of our birth. We feel safe, secure, accepted, and loved. Throughout a woman's lifetime there are many intimate relationships crucial to living a life of balance and health emotionally, physically, and spiritually. This includes intimacy with our parents, our spouses, our children, our friends, and our God.

True intimacy can only be experienced when you open your deepest, most intimate, and truest parts to another. In the context of marriage, sexual intimacy is only achieved when you make yourself totally

vulnerable to your spouse. In that meeting of body, mind, and soul, you and your spouse become "one."

When a woman understands this dynamic, she will experience the most powerful form of communication possible between people—intimacy!

In his book *Intimacy*, author Douglas Weiss says: "Intimacy is really not a mystery at all—it is a process."[1] Just as the process of eating right and exercising keeps you healthy and balanced in your physical life, the process of mastering the basic skills of intimacy will allow you to enjoy satisfying and enduring intimacy with your spouse and with others with whom you share an intimate relationship.

We live in a physical world, and as physical beings we crave physical intimacy. In a Harvard Medical School study, researchers discovered that physical touch is the key to bonding between infants and their mothers. They found that institutionalized children in the orphanages of Romania, whose caregivers offered no physical touch, did not form normal relationships with other kids and were unresponsive and fearful. They exhibited behaviors such as self-clasping, rocking, and swaying.[2]

> *Dr. Janet's Recommendation:*
>
> Take time out to keep your marriage exciting. Plan daily, weekly, and weekend "dates" to keep the spark alive.

The research demonstrated crucial links among touch, the secretion of the stress hormone cortisol, and social development. Abnormal cortisol levels in the children of Romania were found to interfere with their growth and mental and motor activities. The researchers were able to observe this same finding among victims of the Holocaust, severely depressed people, and those with post-traumatic stress disorder.[3]

Touch is so much a part of physical intimacy. Douglas Weiss says, "This is especially true in a marriage. A couple who regularly touches one another by holding hands, hugging, kissing, and giving an occasional pat on the back has mastered the much-needed nonsexual physical intimacy."[4]

Emotional intimacy "engages the soul, touching, connecting, and finding a place of security and permanence in the other where you can rest."[5] The capacity for deepening intimacy with your spouse and loved ones is endless. But one of the first steps we need to take to share emotional intimacy with another is to learn to identify our own real emotions. To share emotional intimacy with another, you must learn to share yourself.

Intimacy is not only expressed by touch. Intimacy can be expressed many ways. Tell your parents, your children, and your friends that you love and care for them. Then show them on a daily basis. Tell your spouse how much you love him, and constantly show him. Make time for sexual, recreational, and social time together.

## INTIMACY 101

A healthy emotional self is imperative to intimacy. It is our emotions that allow us to enjoy fulfilling and heartfelt intimacy with others. I have listed the most common issues that make intimacy an impossibility.

## ROADBLOCKS TO INTIMACY

### Pride

Low self-esteem produces false pride, envy, anger, prejudice, resentment, and arrogance. False pride is usually born out of fear, self-doubt, and anger. A woman, when full of pride, can become heavily burdened with fear and self-doubt and angrily rebel against these traits by adopting a superior attitude, making intimacy impossible.

### Envy

Low self-esteem and an unforgiving, resentful nature are associated with envy. As a woman, you need to know that God made you with unique and special attributes that are an expression of Him. You are valuable; you are loved. Envy can keep you trapped in a life that prevents you from God's abundance and the joy of intimacy with others.

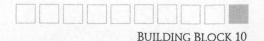

*Anger*

Anger is one of the biggest roadblocks to intimacy. When you allow anger to fester within, it causes pain, and it can lead to physical disease and isolation.

## Dr. Janet's Remedy for Intimacy Roadblocks

- Learn to control your emotions.
- Do not overreact.
- Take responsibility for your own emotional self.
- Forgive once and for all.
- Surround yourself with positive and uplifting people.
- Open your heart without any expectations.
- Love, love, love! Love, and allow yourself to be loved.

## A WOMAN IN COMMUNITY

When it comes to your parents, your children, and your closest friends, the act of giving yourself to these relationships reveals and conveys who you are, and it allows you to express yourself in open, authentic, and vulnerable community.

As women we are all members of a community of care. Volunteering and community service are associated with improved health. Many women feel a sense of belonging when they give to others. Some women feel that the more they do, the more acceptance they will get. This can be dangerous in terms of your health. You must learn the difference between overcare and care. True care of others, coming from unconditional love, will enhance your health, while overcare and resultant burnout from not delegating responsibility will ultimately destroy your health and run your batteries down.

I have personally experienced this. To be forewarned is to be forearmed. I did not listen to the whispers my body kept giving me. Finally,

I was "hit over the head" with a serious stress-related illness. Again, from my heart to yours, you have to ask yourself: *What motivates my overdoing or overcaring?* Is it truly unconditional love? If so, that is fine. Just make sure that you also take care of you in the process. Remember the essentials of caring for yourself: sleep enough, eat properly, exercise, drink plenty of water, and enjoy friends and the community.

But on the other hand, if your caregiving is motivated by fear, you must take a hard look at where that fear is rooted. Could it be that you give to the point of physical and emotional exhaustion just to feel accepted and loved? If so, you are setting yourself up for martyrdom. It is healthy for both the recipient and the giver when you bring comfort to someone, but many women have paid the price for giving of themselves when they had run out of their own reserves. Personal illness is a great teacher.

> *Dr. Janet's Recommendation:*
> Water your friendships—they are flowers in the garden of life!

My message to you is this: as women, we cannot be available to someone in a healthy way unless we are attending to our own needs and having them met. This may seem selfish at first, but in the long run, you will be stronger, healthier, and, believe it or not, better equipped to care for others. It is like putting the oxygen mask over your own nose first so that you can help everyone else around you! While you care for others in your community, you must care for yourself and your soul.

### The importance of community

Studies show that the fewer human connections we have at home, at work, and in the community, the more likely we are to get sick, flood our brains with anxiety-causing chemicals, and die prematurely. In groundbreaking studies of seven thousand people in California, those with the fewest connections to family, friends, community, and religious institutions were three times more likely to die over the nine years in which the study was conducted.[6] Most interesting was that those who had the most connections lived significantly longer, even if they smoked, drank, or lived on bacon cheeseburgers. According to psychiatrist Edward M.

Hallowell, author of *Connect*, "Connectedness is as much a protective factor, probably more than lowering your blood pressure, losing weight, quitting smoking, or wearing your seatbelt." He goes on to say, "It's the unacknowledged key to emotional and physical health, and that's medical fact."[7]

According to Mark Leary, PhD, of Wake Forest University in Winston-Salem, North Carolina, longing for stable relationships is a fundamental human need that has only two requirements: regular contact, and persistent demonstrations of caring.[8] With every heartbeat, we need to feel that we belong. The need for acceptance is built in, down to the marrow of our bones. In other words, friendship is not a luxury; it is a necessity.

In today's world the bonding practice of female connectedness is often replaced by technology. It has become easier and easier to order products and services online, to communicate via e-mail, and to transact all our business from our computers in our homes. It is important to our current and future health to reconnect with our friends and our community because, as I stated previously, it has been proven that the more human connections we have, the more likely we are to live longer and live better.

## A WOMAN AND HER GOD

Make time each day to commune with God. Share your deepest feelings with your heavenly Father. In Him you have ultimate intimacy. According to Linda C. Grenz and Delbert C. Glover in *The Marriage Journey*, the sexual relationship we share with our spouse is closely related to our spirituality.[9] Spending time building sexual intimacy with our spouse contributes to our spiritual life as well, moving us beyond mere intercourse to being deeply and fully "one" with our spouse. This brings us into that space where at some deep level, we are aware of being "one" with God.

True intimacy is the garden of life; you must water it, fertilize it, nurture it, and look upon it with joy! When it comes to our spiritual selves, God is our intimate partner. A woman's relationship with her Creator impacts her body, mind, emotions, and spirit.

As women, we deal with the empty-nest syndrome, marriages that need constant watering, aging parents, hormonal imbalances, stress, and much more. You must rely on faith now more than ever, but at the same time be proactive in terms of your health. Life without balance is merely an existence. An existence with balance is truly a life!

Many women invest their whole lives in a man. Now, while it is true that a man can be your lover and companion, he cannot be your Lord. A man cannot heal your hurt or pain. Men need healing, too. Women need to take feelings of unforgiveness and unresolved issues to God. As T. D. Jakes states in *The Lady, Her Lover, and Her Lord*, "We may be others' nurses or assistants, but we cannot perform the surgery. We all are at best, just helpers. The detailed craftsmanship must come from the Master."[10] He goes on to say that God is the Great Comforter. "He can unravel the dark shroud of grief and release the captive heart that is buried within. He has the ability to wipe away trauma and restore peace. He catches out tears and collects our pains."[11]

> *Dr. Janet's Recommendation:*
>
> When it comes to achieving balance, a woman's soul demands as much attention as the body. It demands fellowship and communion with God. It demands worship, quietness, and meditation.

Just as a woman's body has certain characteristics or appetites, so does her soul. Her soul longs for peace, contentment, and happiness. Her soul has an appetite for God. She yearns to be reconciled to God and have fellowship with Him forever.

Many times when a woman suffers from anxiety, depression, stress, and resultant physical illness, spiritual depletion takes place. The following chart will help you to deal with these symptoms, especially with depression.

## 🍃 Dr. Janet's Protocol for Depression

*Natural support for depression*

- ↪ B-complex vitamins
- ↪ Vitamin B$_6$: needed to manufacture serotonin
- ↪ Vitamin B$_{12}$: helps the brain make acetylcholine, a neurotransmitter involved in learning and memory
- ↪ Folic acid: needed to make mood elevators called *catecholamines*, such as dopamine, norepinephrine, and epinephrine[12]

The following supplements have been shown to aid in the management of depression. It is recommended that you choose only one at a time so that you can see how well you respond. (Note: If you are already on a doctor-prescribed antidepressant, do not stop treatment without consulting your physician. Stopping abruptly can cause withdrawal symptoms such as tremors, vomiting, nausea, fatigue, and headache, not to mention a reemergence of depression.)

- ↪ SAMe, 400 mg, has been a blessing to depression sufferers, relieving both depression and pain in many instances.
- ↪ St. John's wort is a natural antidepressant. Take 300 mg three times daily. It should not be taken in conjunction with SSRI medications.
- ↪ 5-HTP (5-hydroxytryptophan) naturally increases serotonin levels (natural Prozac). It is important in the formation of neurotransmitters in the brain. It should not be taken in conjunction with SSRI medications.
- ↪ CoQ$_{10}$ stimulates immunity and helps decrease immunodeficiency in times of chronic anxiety, depression, and grief.
- ↪ Omega-3 fatty acids
- ↪ Ginkgo biloba
- ↪ Ginseng
- ↪ Phenylalanine
- ↪ Tyrosine (Note: If you are taking a MAO inhibitor medication, you *should not* use tyrosine because it can raise your blood pressure.)
- ↪ DMAE

- L-carnitine
- Thyroxine (if thyroid function is low). This amino acid is excellent for people who have prolonged and intense stress.

Proper nutrition is crucial and is key to your brain's behavior. Eat foods that are rich in calcium, magnesium, and B vitamins. Eat foods that contain tryptophan, such as turkey, potatoes, and bananas. Remember to cut out sugary foods and caffeine, and drink pure water only. Feed your brain a mixture of lecithin, wheat germ, and brewer's yeast (take 2–3 tablespoons daily). Sprinkle it on oatmeal or your favorite whole-grain cereal.

However, you cannot overcome these symptoms and achieve full balance through merely following a protocol for physical relief. I have included this chapter to impress upon you that if you neglect the spiritual part of your being, balance is not possible. More than three hundred studies have confirmed that people of faith are healthier than nonbelievers and are less likely to die prematurely from any cause. Having faith can also speed recovery from physical and mental illness, surgery, and addiction. Faith gives you a sense of peace and an ability to help you look beyond your present problems with hope, which in turn reduces stress and lowers your risk of anxiety and depression.

For many women, the church is a place where they feel part of a community of people who care and take an interest in their lives. This translates into a feeling of connectedness and increased feelings of meaning and purpose. According to Dale A. Matthews, MD, an associate professor of medicine at Georgetown University School of Medicine in Washington DC and the author of *The Faith Factor: Proof of the Healing Power of Prayer,* the body responds positively to faith.[13] Blood pressure and pulse rate tend to be lower, oxygen consumption better, brain wave patterns slower, and immune function enhanced if you practice your faith regularly. When you realize that you are a spiritual being having an earthly experience, you will then understand the importance of feeding your soul as part of balancing your body and regenerating your life.

BUILDING BLOCK 10

## BALANCE IN INTIMACY

If you are a woman who is suffering from imbalance of body, mind, and spirit, it is my prayer that this book will help to bring you back to the point of balance. It is only then that you can be the true expression of what God intended you to be. In order to fulfill the divine destiny that He chose for you even before you were in your mother's womb, you must know that this can only be accomplished when you are whole, healed, and free. (See Psalm 139:13–16.)

When you lose your balance, it forces you into self-examination. It forces you to take a deeper look at your life. Old rooted beliefs have to be unearthed and discarded if they have contributed to imbalance in your life. And, maybe, for the first time unbelief is challenged or replaced by a deepened faith in God.

You still need to take care of your physical body. Devote quality time to your relationships and focus on all other aspects of body balance needing attention that were discussed in previous chapters.

There seems to be two distinct groups of women, *victims* and *survivors*. Both groups may have experienced the same amount of disappointment, sorrow, and pain in their lives, but their views on their experiences are dramatically different. A woman in the victim role is paralyzed by the past and unable to forgive and move forward. Balance eludes her. On the other hand, a woman who is a survivor has learned from her past and uses it to propel her and inspire her to make lifestyle changes necessary with the wisdom gained and the spiritual growth experienced to continue on with faith and hope as traveling companions.

Taking steps to regain your balance—body, mind, and spirit—will transform you, especially when you seek spiritual transformation by strengthening your relationship with God. It is a regeneration that surpasses the physical regeneration mentioned earlier in chapter one. This is because, as I have stated before, we are spiritual beings having a human experience. Regeneration and restoration by the grace of God are like a woman coming home to herself. Her spirit knows it. She delights in the comfort she receives from fellowship with God.

Thousands, if not millions, of American women have lost their balance. You are not the first. You now are arming yourself with the tools needed to regain a vibrant life. Will you rise and meet the challenge?

# CHAPTER 12

# BALANCE AT A GLANCE

Here you are at the end of your body-balancing journey. It is my prayer that you feel confident and armed with the tools and education needed in order to experience a balanced life.

## THE KEYS TO BALANCE

- *Know your body*: Access your current health status by taking the eight-system health screening.
- *Nutritional balance*: Nourish your body with proper nutrition.
- *Vitamins and supplements*: Balance your system using nutrients that are specific for detoxifying, balancing, and strengthening your system.
- *Weight control*: Manage stress eating. Use fat-burning herbs, and eat with balance. Address thyroid health.
- *Exercise*: Commit to thirty minutes of exercise daily, including aerobic exercise, strength training, and stretching exercises.
- *Sleep*: Make a conscious effort to avoid sleep deprivation. It is vital to your well-being.
- *Beauty*: Cultivate beauty—body, mind, and spirit.

THE TEN ESSENTIAL BUILDING BLOCKS

- *Antiaging*: Choose to adopt a positive attitude about the aging process. Have yearly health screenings, and take antiaging supplements.
- *Hormones*: Have yearly hormonal assays performed to determine your hormonal status. Then take steps to achieve balance.
- *Stress reduction*: Address your emotional health, and develop a strong spiritual life.
- *Relationships*: Water all relationships. Forgive, trust, and love.

As a woman, you are blessed with many milestones that are unique to femininity. The birth of a child; the day your daughter gives birth, along with the double blessing of becoming a grandmother; the experience of menopause, which gives birth to your wise woman years; the hormonal changes that bring you to resolution, peace, and the healing of your past unfinished business—all are events to be celebrated and cherished. You can only fully experience all of these events when your life is one of balance.

The biggest gift that you can give to yourself and others is a balanced YOU!

# DISCLAIMER

Dr. Maccaro is prohibited from addressing a patient's medical condition by phone, facsimile, or e-mail. Please refer questions related to your medical condition to your health-care provider.

The following books and authors have been instrumental in bringing outstanding information in regard to emotional, dietary, and lifestyle links to disease and mental unrest. Their work is inspirational and will have a profound influence on your life.

Airola, Paavo. *Every Woman's Book*. Arizona: Health Plus Publishers, 1979.

Foster, Helen. *The Beauty Book*. United Kingdom: Parragon Publishing, 2002.

*The Lark Letter*, Phillips Health LLC, 2003, featuring Susan Lark, MD. To order the *Lark Letter*, call (877) 437-5275.

Lee, John R., MD, Jesse Hanley, MD, and Virginia Hopkins. *What Your Doctor May Not Tell You About Premenopause*. New York: Warner Books, 1999.

Maccaro, Janet, PhD, CNC. *Breaking the Grip of Dangerous Emotions*. Lake Mary, FL: Siloam, 2001, 2005.

_____. *Midlife Meltdown*. Lake Mary, FL: Siloam, 2004.

_____. *Natural Health Remedies*. Lake Mary, FL: Siloam, 2003, 2006.

_____. *90-Day Immune System Makeover*. Lake Mary, FL: Siloam, 2000, 2006.

Northrup, Christiane. *The Wisdom of Menopause*. New York, Bantam Books, 2001.

Page, Linda, PhD. *Healthy Healing*. N.p.: Traditional Wisdom, Inc., 2000.

Perricone, Nicholas, MD. *The Perricone Promise: Look Younger, Live Longer in Three Easy Steps*. New York: Warner Books, 2004.

Reichman, Judith, MD. *Relax, This Won't Hurt*. New York: William Morrow and Co., Inc., 2000.

Turner, Kevin Lane. *A Journey to the Other Side of Life*. N.p.: Ashley Down Publishing Co., 1995.

Wilson, James L., ND, DC, PhD. *Adrenal Fatigue, the 21st Century Stress Syndrome*. Petaluma, CA: Smart Publications, 2001.

## INTRODUCTION

1. Christiane Northrup, MD, *Mother-Daughter Wisdom* (New York: Bantam, 2005), back cover matter.

## CHAPTER 1 • KNOW YOUR BODY

1. DicQie Fuller, PhD, DSc, *The Healing Power of Enzymes* (New York: Forbes, Inc., 1998), 118.

2. *Stop Improper Digestion, Renew Life*; 2076 Sunnydale Blvd, Clearwater, FL 33765.

3. "Gallbladder Disease," Merck Source Resource Library, http://www .mercksource.com/pp/us/cns/cns_hl_adam.jspzQzpgzEzzSzppdocszSzuszSzcnsz SzcontentzSzadamzSzencyzSzarticlezSz001138zPz.htm (accessed March 27, 2006).

4. "Migraine," National Headache Foundation, Educational Resources, http:// www.headaches.org/consumer/topicsheets/migraine.html (accessed March 27, 2006).

5. "What Are High Blood Pressure and Prehypertension?" *Your Guide to Lowering Blood Pressure,* http://www.nhlbi.nih.gov/hbp/hbp/whathbp.htm (accessed March 27, 2006).

6. Linda Page, *Healthy Healing,* 11th ed. (N.p.: Traditional Wisdom, Inc., 2000), 324.

7. Janet Maccaro, *Natural Health Remedies* (Lake Mary, FL: Siloam, 2003, 2006), 114–115.

8. Adapted from Health Education AIDS Liaison, Toronto, "Steven James' Totally Subjective Nonscientific Guide to Illness and Health," Ten Step Programs, http://www.healtoronto.com/tenstep.html (accessed March 27, 2006), from *Surviving and Thriving With AIDS: Hints for the Newly Diagnosed,* copyright © 1987, People With AIDS Coalition, Inc.

9. Kevin Lane Turner, *A Journey to the Other Side of Life* (United Kingdom: Ashley Down Publishing Company, 1995).

10. Ibid.

11. Janet Maccaro, *Breaking the Grip of Dangerous Emotions* (Lake Mary, FL: Siloam, 2001, 2005), 131.

12. Irene S. Levine, "Antidepressants: Too Much of a Good Thing?" *USA Today,* http://www.usatoday.com/news/health/2002-10-17-antidepressants_x.htm (accessed June 12, 2006).

13. Depression FAQs, "Does depression affect males, females, or both?" Athealth.com, http://www.athealth.com/Consumer/disorders/Depression.html (accessed June 12, 2006).

14. Dick Tibbits, "Hypertension Reduction Through Forgiveness Training,"

ACPE Research Newsletters, http://www.acperesearch.net/Winter02.html (accessed March 31, 2006).

15. "The Numbers Count: Mental Disorders in America," National Institute of Health, rev. 2006, http://www.nimh.nih.gov/publicat/numbers.cfm#Dysthymic (accessed June 12, 2006).

16. James Allen, *As a Man Thinketh*, in *The Wisdom of James Allen*, five classic works combined into one (San Diego, CA: Laurel Creek Press, 1997), 38–39.

17. Dale A. Matthews, *The Faith Factor: Proof of the Healing Power of Prayer* (New York: Penguin, 1991), 109–110.

18. Ibid.

## CHAPTER 2 • NUTRITIONAL BALANCE:
## BUILDING BLOCK 1

1. Susan Lark and James Richards, *The Chemistry of Success* (San Francisco, CA: Bay Books, 2000).

2. Janet Maccaro, *90-Day Immune System Makeover* (Lake Mary, FL: Siloam, 2000, 2006), 203–204.

3. Ibid., 205–206.

4. For more information about Penta water, visit the research studies at http://www.pentawater.com/research.shtml.

5. Phyllis Balch, *Rx Prescription for Cooking & Dietary Wellness* (New York: PAB Books, Inc., 1992).

6. "Prevention Makes Common Cents," U.S. Department of Health and Human Services, http://aspe.hhs.gov/health/prevention/index.shtml#DIABETES (accessed on March 28, 2006).

7. Linda L. Prout, *Live in the Balance: The Ground-Breaking East-West Nutrition Program* (New York: Marlowe and Company, 2000), 213.

8. Page, *Healthy Healing*, 11th ed., 170.

9. H. J. Roberts, *Aspartame: Is It Safe?* (Philadelphia, PA: Charles Press Publishers, 1990).

10. James Bowen, MD, "Aspartame Murders Infants, Violates Federal Genocide Law," http://www.wnho.net/aspartame_murders_infants.htm (accessed March 28, 2006).

11. Linda Page, *Healthy Healing*, 12th ed. (Del Ray Oaks, CA: Healthy Healing Publications, 2004), 152.

12. "Health Benefits of Stevia," http://reid_j.tripod.com/stevia.htm (accessed March 28, 2006).

13. This section on candida is adapted from my book *Natural Health Remedies*, pages 129–131.

14. William Crook, *The Yeast Connection* (London: Vintage, 1986).

15. Ibid.

16. Maccaro, *90-Day Immune System Makeover*, 103.

17. Phyllis Balch and James Balch, *Prescription for Nutritional Healing* (New York: Avery Publishing Group, 2000).

## CHAPTER 3 • THE WORLD OF VITAMINS AND SUPPLEMENTS: BUILDING BLOCK 2

1. *New Beauty*, Winter/Spring 2005, 38.

2. Robert Atkins, MD, *Dr. Atkins New Diet Revolution*, revised and updated (New York: M. Evans and Company, Inc., 1999), 76.

3. Christopher Hobbs, *Medicinal Mushrooms* (United Kingdom: Culinary Arts, Ltd., 1995).

4. *Energy Times*, November/December 1999; *Townsend Letter*, June 1998; Paul Stamets, *Growing Gourmet and Medicinal Mushrooms* (N.p.: Ten Speed Publishing, 1994).

5. Janet Maccaro, *Natural Health Remedies* (Lake Mary, FL: Siloam, 2003, 2006), 11–20.

## CHAPTER 4 • GUIDELINES TO WEIGHT CONTROL: BUILDING BLOCK 3

1. Taken from "Ten Steps to Healthy Weight," *Health Magazine*, January/February 1998.

2. *New Beauty*, Winter/Spring 2005, 38.

3. "The Hamilton Anxiety Scale (HAMA)," The Anxiety Community, http://www.anxietyhelp.org/information/hama.html (accessed March 31, 2006).

4. "Conjugated Linoleic Acid Fights Cancer, Heart Disease, and More," *Life Enhancement*, http://www.life-enhancement.com/article_template.asp?ID=613 (accessed June 13, 2006).

5. Ibid.

6. Rena R. Wing and Robert W. Jeffery, "Benefits of Recruiting Participants With Friends and Increasing Social Support for Weight Loss and Maintenance," *Journal of Consulting and Clinical Psychology* 67 (February 1999): 132–138.

7. E. S. Epel, et al., "Stress and Body Shape: Stress-Induced Cortisol Secretion Is Consistently Greater Among Women With Central Fat," *Psychosomatic Medicine* 62 (September 2000): 623–632. See also *Life Extension*, December 2005.

## CHAPTER 5 • THE IMPORTANCE OF EXERCISE: BUILDING BLOCK 4

1. Mike George, *Learn to Relax, a Practical Guide* (San Francisco: Chronicle Books, 1998), 62–63.

2. M. Haji Faraji and A. H. Jaji Tarkhani, "The Effect of Sour Tea (*Hibiscus sabdariffa*) on Essential Hypertension," *Journal of Ethnopharmacology* 65 (June 1999): 231–236.

3. "Making Your Heart Rate Count," Jacki's Aerobic Programs SuperSite, http://www.jackis.com/Heart_Rates.htm (accessed June 14, 2006). Used courtesy of Jacki Sorensen's Aerobic Programs.

4. Fitness Tool: Target Heart Rate Calculator, http://www.mayoclinic.com/health/target-heart-rate/SM00083 (accessed June 14, 2006).

5. "Growing Stronger—Strength Training for Older Adults: Why Strength Training?" Division of Nutrition and Physical Activity, National Center for Disease Prevention and Health Promotion, http://www.cdc.gov/nccdphp/dnpa/physical /growing_stronger/why.htm (accessed April 4, 2006).

6. The Exercise and Physical Fitness Page, Department of Kinesiology and Health, Georgia State University, http://www2.gsu.edu/~wwwfit/strength.html (accessed April 4, 2006).

7. The Major Muscle Groups, Strength Training Basics, http://www.primusweb .com/fitnesspartner/library/activity/trainbasics.htm (accessed April 4, 2006).

8. "Improve Your Flexibility With a Good Stretching Program," Stretching Basics, Sport Medicine, http://sportsmedicine.about.com/cs/flexibility/a/aa040703a .htm (accessed April 4, 2006).

9. Ibid.

10. Ibid.

### CHAPTER 6 • SLEEP—THE PAUSE THAT REFRESHES: BUILDING BLOCK 5

1. M. W. Johns, "A New Method for Measuring Daytime Sleepiness: The Epworth Sleepiness Scale," *Sleep* 14 (1991): 540–545. Copyright © M. W. Johns, 1990–1997. Reproduced with permission.

2. "Symptoms of Sleep Deprivation," http://nurseweb.villanova.edu/womenwith disabilities/sleep/slpdep.htm (accessed March 29, 2006).

3. "Good Sleep, Good Learning, Good Life," http://www.supermemo.com /articles/sleep.htm#Sleep%20deprivation%20in%20the%society (accessed March 29, 2006).

4. "Sleep Deprivation," Better Health Channel, http://www.betterhealth.vic.gov .au/bhcv2/bhcarticles.nsf/pages/Sleep_deprivation?OpenDocument (accessed March 29, 2006).

5. E. U. Vorbach, R. Gortelmeyer, and J. Bruining, "Therapy for Insomnia: Efficacy and Tolerability of a Valerian Preparation, 600 mg of Valerian," *Psychopharmakotherapie* 3 (1996): 109–115.

6. Sally Squires, "Back to Basics," *Washington Post*, September 25, 2001, F1.

### CHAPTER 7 • TRUE BEAUTY—NATURALLY: BUILDING BLOCK 6

1. "The Hazards of Smoking," Quit Smoking and Herbal Detox Program, TheHerbDoc.com, http://www.theherbdoc.com/programs/Smoking.htm (accessed June 15, 2006).

2. "Nicotinamide: Golden Thread in the Tapestry of Life," LifeEnhancement .com, http://www.life-enhancement.com/article_template.asp?ID=484 (accessed June 15, 2006).

3. Helen Foster, *The Complete Beauty Book* (United Kingdom: Parragon Publishing, 2002), 24; see also *New Beauty*, Florida Edition, Summer/Fall 2005, 81.

4. Maccaro, *Natural Health Remedies*, 64.

5. Ibid., 25–26.

6. Adapted from Foster, *The Complete Beauty Book*, 189.

7. *New Beauty*, Winter/Spring 2005, 38.

## CHAPTER 8 • AN ANTIAGING PROTOCOL:
## BUILDING BLOCK 7

1. Louise Hawkley, senior research scientist with the Center for Cognitive and Social Neuroscience at the University of Chicago, and John Cacioppo, the Tiffany and Margaret Blake Distinguished Service Professor in Psychology, cited in "Evidence Mounts of Dire Consequence of Loneliness for Older Americans," SeniorJournal.com, http://www.seniorjournal.com/NEWS/Aging/6-03-28 -EvidenceMounts.htm (accessed March 29, 2006).

2. Ibid.

3. "Successful Aging is Simply 'Mind over Matter' Says New Study," Senior Journal.com, http://www.seniorjournal.com/NEWS/Aging/5-12-12 -AgingMindOverMatter.htm (accessed March 29, 2006).

4. "People Age Better If Happy and Free of Negative Images of Aging," SeniorJournal.com, at http://www.seniorjournal.com/NEWS/Aging/4-09 -13HappyAging.htm (accessed March 29, 2006).

5. This chart has been adapted from "Health Screenings for Women," Saint Joseph Regional Medical Center, Health Topics Library, http://healthlibrary.epnet .com/search.aspx?token=48ce1b7c-a108-4c7a-bdb9-14f3725ef0a9 (accessed April 6, 2006).

6. Shiow Wang, PhD, Plant Physiologist, USDA Agricultural Research Service, Beltsville, Maryland, http://www.ghorganics.com/Mexican%20Oregano%20Tops .htm (accessed March 29, 2006).

7. *New Beauty*, Winter/Spring 2005, 38.

8. Janet Maccaro, *Midlife Meltdown* (Lake Mary, FL: Siloam, 2004), 40.

9. This antiaging protocol was adapted from: James F. Balch, MD, Mark Stengler, ND, *IMPAKT, Health/Delicious Living* magazine, 2004; and James F. Balch, MD, Mark Stengler, ND, *Prescription for Natural Cures* (New York: John Wiley and Sons, Inc., 2004).

## CHAPTER 9 • HARMONIZING HORMONES:
## BUILDING BLOCK 8

1. *New Beauty*, Winter/Spring 2005, 38.

2. Guy E. Abraham, MD, and Ruth E. Rumley, MD, "Role of Nutrition in Managing the Premenstrual Tension Syndromes," *Journal of Reproductive Medicine* 32(6) (June 1987): accessed at http://www.mgwater.com/gapmts.shtml on March 31, 2006.

3. John R. Lee, MD, with Jesse Hanley and Virginia Hopkins, *What Your Doctor May Not Tell You About Premenopause* (New York: Warner Books, 1999), 60.

4. Ibid.

5. Ibid.

6. Eldred B. Taylor, MD, Medical Director, Department of Integrative Medicine, Dekalb Medical Center, Atlanta, Georgia, http://www.taylormedicalgroup.net.

7. Sylvia Wassertheil-Smoller, et al., "Effect of Estrogen Plus Progestin on Stroke in Postmenopausal Women: The Woman's Health Initiative: A Randomized Trial," *Journal of the American Medical Association* 289 (May 28, 2003): 2673–2684.

8. D. C. Smith, et al., "Association of Exogenous Estrogen and Endometrial Carcinoma," *New England Journal of Medicine* 293(23) (1975): 1164–1167.

9. Collaborative Group on Hormonal Factors in Breast Cancer, "Breast Cancer and Hormone Replacement Therapy: Collaborative Reanalysis of Data From 51 Epidemiological Studies of 52,705 Women With Breast Cancer and 108,411 Women Without Breast Cancer," *Lancet* 350 (October 11, 1997): 1047–1059.

10. Catherine Schairer, et al., "Menopausal Estrogen and Estrogen-Progestin Replacement and Breast Cancer Risk," *Journal of the American Medical Association* 283 (January 26, 2000): 485–491.

11. "A Review of the Effectiveness of *Cimicifuga Racemosa* (Black Cohosh) for the Symptoms of Menopause," *Journal of Women's Health* 7 (June 1998): 525–529. See also A. Petho, "28 Women Were Able to Make the Switch in a Clinical Study to Black Cohosh Without Being Given Additional Hormones," and "Menopausal Complaints: Changeover of a Hormone Treatment to an Herbal Gynecological Remedy Practicable?" *Arzliche Praxis* 38 (1987): 1551–1553.

12. Don Gambrell, R. C. Maier, and R. Sanders, "Decreased Incidence of Breast Cancer in Postmenopausal Estrogen-Progesterone Users," *O. B. Gynecol* 62 (1983): 435–443. See also: "Osteoporosis: Osteoporosis Renewal: The Role of Progesterone," *Int. Clin. Nutr.* 10 (1990): 384–391. See also: O. Picazo and A. Fernandez-Guasti, "Anti-Anxiety Effects of Progesterone and Some of Its Reduced Metabolites. An Evaluation Using the Burying Behavior Test," *Byain Res.* 680 (1995): 13541. See also: J. C. Prior, "Bone Loss: Progesterone as a Bone Trophic Hormone," *Endocrine Revs.* 11 (1990): 306–308.

## CHAPTER 10 • REDUCING STRESS:
## BUILDING BLOCK 9

1. "Health Reports: Stress and Chronic Conditions, Excess Weight and Arthritis," *The Daily*, January 21, 2004, http://www.statcan.ca/Daily/English/040121 /d040121b.htm (accessed March 29, 2006).

2. Ibid.

3. This inventory and plan of attack was adapted from J. Coudert, *Advice From a Failure* (New York: Stein and Day, 1983); M. Beattie, *The Language of Letting Go* (New York: Harper Collins, 1990), 84; and J. D. Quick and R. Horn, "Health Consequences of Stress," Special Issue, *Journal of Organizational Behavior Management* 8 (1986): 19–36.

4. Developed by Mary A. Fristad, PhD, Psychologist, Director of Research and Psychological Services in the Division of Child and Adolescent Psychiatry at the Ohio State University Medical Center. E-mail address: fristad.1@osu.edu, accessed at http://faculty.psy.ohio-state.edu/1/fristad/ on March 31, 2006.

5. *Natural Health*, November/December 1998, 168–172.

6. Ray Sahelian, MD, *5-HTP: Nature's Serotonin Solution* (New York: Avery Publishing Group, 1998).

7. Maccaro, *Midlife Meltdown*, 135–136.

8. *New Beauty,* Winter/Spring 2005, 38.

9. "Adrenal Function and Ascorbic Acid Concentrations in Elderly Women," *Gerontology* (Switzerland) 24(6) (1978): 473–476.

10. J. R. Thomas, et al., "Tyrosine Improves Working Memory in a Multitasking Environment," *Pharmacol, Biochem. Behav.* 64 (November 1999): 495–500.

11. R. Bernardine and L. DeAmbrosi, "Pharmacodynamic Properties of Adrenal Cortical Extracts in Comparison to Synthetic Corticosteriod Mixture in the Rat," *Arch. Int. Pharmacodyn. Ther.* 276 (August 1985).

## CHAPTER 11 • A WOMAN'S RELATIONSHIPS: BUILDING BLOCK 10

1. Douglas Weiss, *Intimacy—the 100 Day Guide to Lasting Relationships* (Lake Mary, FL: Siloam, 2001, 2003), 2.

2. William J. Cromie, "Of Hugs and Hormones," *Harvard University Gazette,* http://www.news.harvard.edu/gazette/1998/06.11/OfHugsandHormon.html (accessed March 30, 2006).

3. Ibid.

4. Weiss, *Intimacy,* 30.

5. Ibid., 17.

6. Edward M. Hallowell, MD, *Connect: 12 Vital Ties That Open Your Heart, Lengthen Your Life, and Deepen Your Soul* (New York: Pantheon, 1999).

7. Ibid.

8. Hara Estroff Marano, "Friends for Life," *American Health,* February 1999, 55–56.

9. Linda C. Grenz and Delbert D. Glover, *The Marriage Journey* (Boston, MA: Cowley Publications, 1996).

10. T. D. Jakes, *The Lady, Her Lover, and Her Lord* (New York: Putnam Adult, 1998), 204.

11. Ibid.

12. "Depression," LifeExtension.org, http://www.lef.org/protocols/prtcls-txt /t-prtcl-040.html (accessed June 16, 2006), citing Bukreev, 1978; Carney, et al., 1990; Carney, 1995; Fujii, et al., 1996; Masuda, et al., 1998; Bottiglieri, et al., 2000; Zhao, et al., 2001.

13. Dale A. Matthews, MD, *The Faith Factor: Proof of the Healing Power of Prayer* (New York: Viking Penquin, 1998).

# Visit Dr. Janet's Web site

at www.DrJanetPhD.com
or call 800.231.8485 to order

Dr. Janet's Balanced by Nature Products, including:

- Dr. Janet's Woman's Balance Formula

- Dr. Janet's Skin Cream

- Dr. Janet's Glucosamine Cream

- Dr. Janet's Beach Buffer

- Dr. Janet's Coconut Dream

- Dr. Janet's Safe Passage (menopausal formula)

- Dr. Janet's Tranquility (stress formula)

All other products mentioned in this book can be found at your local health food store.

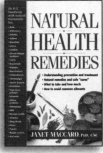
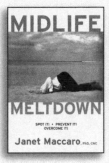